The Chicken Cookbook

Chicken Akademy

Table of Contents

CHICKEN TORTELLINI SOUP	23
SEASONING MIX FOR CHICKEN	24
MARINADE FOR CHICKEN	25
CHINESE CHICKEN SALAD DRESSING	26
CHICKEN CASSEROLE	27
CHICKEN POT PIE	28
MARY'S CHICKEN DISH	29
CHICKEN WITH RICE	30
CHICKEN TIKKA	31
ITALIAN CHICKEN	32
LEMON - PARSLEY CHICKEN BREASTS	33
QUICK CHICKEN	34
SWEET & SOUR CHICKEN	35
CHICKEN CACCIATORE	36
SUNDAY FRIED CHICKEN	37
HONEY BAKED CHICKEN	38
CORDON BLEU	39
BAKED CHICKEN	40
SICILIAN CHICKEN	41
ROAST CHICKEN WITH ALMONDS	42
WALDORF CHICKEN	43
ORIENTAL CHICKEN	44
CHICKEN YUM YUM!	45
CHICKEN IN ORANGE SAUCE	46
CHICKEN AND RICE	47
CHICKEN PILAF	48
POTTED CHICKEN WITH PEPPERS AND MUSHROOMS	49
MARINATED CHICKEN	50
CHICKEN KABOBS	51

RUSSIAN CHICKEN	52
TURKEY DIVAN	53
SCALLOPED CHICKEN	54
CHICKEN A LA KING	55
APRICOT CHICKEN	56
BOWL OF THE WIFE OF KIT CARSON	57
CHICKEN A LA WORCESTERSHIRE WINE SAUCE	58
BISCUIT DUMPLINGS	59
CHICKEN AND BROCCOLI WITH RICE	60
CHICKEN AND DUMPLINGS	61
CHICKEN AND RICE ALMONDINE SQUASH	62
CHICKEN BREASTS IN SOUR CREAM	63
CHICKEN IN SOUR CREAM GRAVY	64
CHICKEN BREASTS IN SOUR CREAM WITH MUSHROOMS	65
CHICKEN BREAST WITH HONEY - WINE SAUCE	66
CHICKEN CASSEROLE	67
CHICKEN CASSEROLE	68
CHICKEN ALMOND CASSEROLE	69
CHICKEN CHARDONNAY	70
CHICKEN CURRY	71
CHICKEN ENCHILADAS	72
CHICKEN SHERRY	73
CHICKEN PECAN QUICHE	74
CHICKEN SARONNO	75
CHICKEN WELLINGTON	76
CURRANT SAUCE	77
CHUNKY CHICKEN CASSEROLE	78
CONTINENTAL CHICKEN	79
CREAMY HAM AND CHICKEN MEDLEY	80
CHICKEN FRIED RICE	81
EASY CHICKEN TETRAZZINI	82
THE EYES OF TEXAS SAUSAGE CHICKEN CASSEROLE	83
FRAN'S CHICKEN	84

ANATOMY OF THE CHICKEN   88

ANATOMY OF THE CHICKEN   89

HOW MANY CALORIES IN CHICKEN?   90

HOW MANY CALORIES IN CHICKEN?   91

COOKING METHODS   92

COOKING METHODS   93

QUICK RECIPES   94

3 CHEFS' TIPS   95

TIPS AND TRICKS   96

3 DIPS FOR CHICKEN NUGGETS   100

QUICK RECIPES   101

Recipes

CHICKEN TORTELLINI SOUP

ingredients

- × 2 carrots
- × 1 onion
- × 2 garlic cloves
- × 3 cans cream of chicken soup
- × 6 c. water
- × 1 tsp. oregano
- × 1 tsp. basil
- × 1 pkg. boneless chicken breasts, cut into bite-size pieces 1 bag cheese tortellini
- × 2 boxes frozen broccoli

directions

1. Cook the chicken in a small amount of oil.

2. While the meat is cooking, cut the vegetables and open the cans.

3. Add all of the above ingredients to a large pot, except the tortellini and frozen broccoli.

4. These 2 ingredients are added the last 10 minutes or so before serving so they don't overcook.

5. Simmer the other ingredients for an hour or as long as you like.

6. The soup tastes great with freshly grated Italian cheese and a loaf of Italian or French bread.

SEASONING MIX FOR CHICKEN

ingredients

- × 2 1/2 tsp. salt
- × 1 1/2 tsp. paprika
- × 1 tsp. onion powder
- × 3/4 tsp. savory
- × 1/4 tsp. coriander
- × 3/4 tsp. garlic powder
- × 1/2 tsp. black pepper
- × 1/2 tsp. thyme
- × 1/2 tsp. basil, dried crushed sweet

directions

1. Mix all ingredients well.
2. Makes 2 tablespoons plus 2 teaspoons.

MARINADE FOR CHICKEN

ingredients

- × 1/2 c. shoyu
- × 1/4 c. water
- × 1/3 c. salad oil
- × 2 tbsp. dried minced onion
- × 2 tbsp. sesame seeds
- × 1 tbsp. sugar
- × 1 tsp. ground ginger
- × 1/8 tsp. dried red pepper
- × 3/4 tsp. garlic powder

directions

1. Mix all the above ingredients.

2. Let the chicken parts marinate overnight, turning once or twice to make sure they are fully marinated.

3. Bake in 350-degree oven for 1 hour.

4. If you intend to use a charcoal grill, bake first in the oven for 45 minutes and on the grill for 15 minutes.

5. Place the marinade in a Ziploc bag with the chicken parts. This makes turning easier.

CHINESE CHICKEN SALAD DRESSING

ingredients

- × 2 tsp. sesame oil
- × 2 tbsp. sesame seeds, roasted
- × 2 tbsp. sugar
- × 2 tbsp. mayonnaise
- × 2 tbsp. lemon juice
- × 2 tbsp. oil
- × 2 tbsp. shoyu

directions

1. Combine all ingredients and mix well.

2. Drizzle over salad just before serving.

3. This is also a good marinade to pour over skinless chicken the night before grilling.

4. For the salad, make a green salad, with cooked shredded chicken.

5. Sprinkle the top with dry chow mein noodles.

CHICKEN CASSEROLE

ingredients

- × 6 chicken breasts
- × 2 onions
- × 8 c. water (approximately)
- × 3/4 loaf bread
- × Celery
- × Poultry seasoning
- × 2 tbsp.
- × Melted butter
- × 1 can cream of mushroom soup
- × 1 can cream of chicken soup
Sharp cheese, sliced

directions

1. Boil the chicken breasts with 1 onion in about 8 cups of water until tender.

2. Remove the skin and bones and separate them into pieces. Save the chicken broth.

3. Use a 13 x 9-inch pan (sprayed with Pam).

4. Cut small pieces of bread (about 3/4 of a loaf) and place them in the bottom of the pan.

5. Cut 1 onion finely and place it on top of the bread.

6. Sprinkle celery and poultry seasoning on top. Place the chicken pieces on top.

7. Melt the margarine and pour over the chicken pieces.

8. Combine the mushroom soup, cream of chicken, and pour on top.

9. Cover the top with sharp cheese sliced all over the top.

10. Bake until done.

CHICKEN POT PIE

ingredients

- × 3 lb. chicken
- × 1 can French onion soup
- × 1 lg. carrot
- × 1 lg. celery
- × Flour to thicken gravy Water
- × 1 double crust

directions

1. Preheat the oven to 400 degrees.

2. Simmer whole chicken in water with carrots and celery until done, 1 1/2 to 2 hours.

3. Remove the meat and cut it into small pieces. Refrigerate the chicken and broth separately overnight.

4. The next day, trim the fat from the broth, as well as the carrots and celery.

5. Add the onion soup and bring to a boil.

6. Thicken the sauce with flour paste and water.

7. Strain the sauce to remove the onions.

8. Put the chicken on the base of the base.

9. Pour the sauce on top.

10. Place the top base and bake at 400 degrees for 30 minutes.

MARY'S CHICKEN DISH

ingredients

- × 6 pieces boneless breast of chicken
- × 4 tbsp. olive oil
- × 2 tbsp. butter
- × 1 clove garlic Breadcrumbs
- × 2 eggs
- × 1 bouillon cube
- × 1 can chicken broth
- × 6 slices of Mozzarella cheese

directions

1. Dip the boneless, skinless chicken breast in breadcrumbs and eggs.

2. In a large skillet, heat the olive oil, butter, garlic, and melt the bouillon cube.

3. Make sure to put the heat on low so the oil doesn't burn.

4. When the oil is hot, brown the chicken on both sides in oil, increase the heat so that the chicken is well and browned on both sides, lower the heat and add the chicken broth. Cook over low heat until hot.

5. Add mozzarella cheese to the top of the chicken.

CHICKEN WITH RICE

ingredients

- × 3 to 3 1/2 lbs. chicken, cut into serving pieces
- × 1/4 c. butter or margarine
- × 1 1/2 c. instant rice
- × 1 (10 1/2 oz.) can condensed cream of chicken soup
- × 1 c. water
- × 1 tsp. instant chicken bouillon crystals
- × or 1 chicken bouillon cube

directions

1. Preheat skillet (over medium heat) uncovered.

2. Add butter or margarine and let it melt.

3. Place the chicken pieces in a skillet and brown them on both sides.

4. Spice with salt and pepper.

5. Remove chicken from skillet.

6. Reduce heat to simmer "and add the rice.

7. Combine soup.

CHICKEN TIKKA

ingredients

- × 5/8 c. yogurt
- × 4 crushed garlic cloves
- × 1 1/2 inch fresh ginger, peeled & chopped
- × 1 sm. onion, grated
- × 1 1/2 tsp. chili powder
- × 1 tbsp. ground coriander
- × 1 tsp. salt
- × 4 chicken breasts, skinned & boned
- × 1 lg. onion, thinly sliced into rings
- × 2 lg. tomatoes, sliced
- × 2 tbsp. coriander leaves

directions

1. Combine the first 7 ingredients and set them aside.

2. Cut the chicken into 1-inch cubes.

3. Add to marinade, mix well, cover and chill for 6 hours or overnight.

4. Heat the broiler.

5. Place chicken on skewers or in a roasting pan and grill (or grill) for 5 to 8 minutes, turning occasionally until cooked through.

6. Garnish with onion rings, tomatoes, and coriander leaves and serve. 4 portions.

ITALIAN CHICKEN

ingredients

- × 2/3 c. flour
- × 1 tsp. salt
- × 1/2 c. vegetable oil
- × 1 green pepper
- × 1/2 tsp. pepper
- × 1/2 tsp. garlic salt Sliced onion
- × 1 lg. jar spaghetti sauce
- × Chicken (boneless) breasts, quartered

directions

1. Wash the chicken.

2. Mix the flour, salt, pepper, and garlic.

3. Cover the chicken, brown in oil, and then drain.

4. Top the chicken with bell peppers and onions (sliced).

5. Add sauce on top.

6. Cover and simmer for about 1 hour.

7. Serve with spaghetti.

LEMON – PARSLEY CHICKEN BREASTS

ingredients

- × 2 whole chicken breasts, boned & skinned
- × 1/3 c. white wine
- × 1/3 c. lemon juice
- × 2 cloves fresh minced garlic
- × 3 tbsp. breadcrumbs
- × 2 tbsp. olive oil
- × 1/4 c. parsley, fresh

directions

1. In a measuring cup, combine the wine, lemon juice, and garlic.

2. Pound each breast until 1/4-inch thick and lightly coat with breadcrumbs.

3. Heat the olive oil in a large skillet and brown the chicken, 5 minutes on each side.

4. Stir the wine mixture and pour over the chicken in a skillet.

5. Sprinkle with parsley and simmer for 5 minutes. Serve with the juices from the pan.

QUICK CHICKEN

ingredients

- × 1 can cream of mushroom soup 1 can cream of chicken soup
- × 1 c. milk
- × 5 lbs.
- × Cut up cooked chicken 1 pt. sour cream
- × 1 pkg. Pepperidge Farm stuffing mix

directions

1. Mix soups, sour cream and milk.
2. Add chicken.
3. Mix all ingredients and layer in baking dish alternating with stuffing mix.
4. Bake at 350 degrees for 1 hour.

SWEET & SOUR CHICKEN

ingredients

- × 1 frying chicken
- × 1 tbsp.
- × Melted butter
- × Dash of salt,
- × pepper,
- × ginger
- × 3 celery stalks
- × 1 can pineapple (chunk)
- × 2 tbsp.
- × Brown sugar
- × 3 tbsp. water
- × 1 1/2 tbsp. soy sauce
- × 1 tbsp. vinegar
- × 1 tbsp. cornstarch
- × 1 red pepper (optional)

directions

1. Rinse chicken, place skin side up in oiled pan.
2. Pour melted butter over chicken.
3. Sprinkle chicken with salt, pepper, ginger, diced celery.
4. Bake chicken at 325 degrees for about 20 minutes.
5. Drain pineapple juice into cup.
6. Blend in brown sugar, water, soy sauce, vinegar, cornstarch.
7. Pour mixture over chicken in pan.
8. Top with pineapple chunks and pepper.

CHICKEN CACCIATORE

ingredients

- × 1 pkg. chicken
- × 1/4 c. butter
- × 1/2 c. sherry
- × 15 oz. can stewed tomato bits
- × 1 (6 oz.) can mushrooms
- × 1 pkg. Italian dressing mix
- × 1/4 c. chopped green pepper
- × 1 tsp. Italian seasoning Garlic powder,
- × to taste Bayleaf

directions

1. Boil the chicken until done. Save water (use this to boil rice).

2. Cut the chicken into tiny squares.

3. Brown in butter and sherry.

4. Add tomatoes, mushrooms, Italian dressing mix, green bell pepper, and other seasonings.

5. Bring to a boil and simmer for an hour. Serve over rice.

SUNDAY FRIED CHICKEN

ingredients

- × 1 whole chicken or any combo of chicken pieces
- × 1 to 2 c. of flour for coating
- × Salt and pepper to taste
- × 4 tbsp. butter
- × 4 tbsp. Crisco
- × 2 beaten eggs

directions

1. Wash and dry the chicken parts.
2. Combine the salt, pepper, and flour and coat the chicken.
3. Dip each piece in the egg mixture and brown each side in hot, melted shortening and butter. Lower the heat and cook for about 15 more minutes on each side.
4. Use a heavy iron or aluminum skillet if possible.
5. Remove from the pan and drain on a paper towel.
6. Pour all but 3 tablespoons of fat from the pan and reheat.
7. Add 3 tablespoons of flour to the skillet and stir with the fat until lightly browned.
8. Add 2 cups of milk and a little parsley or parsley flakes and cook over medium heat until thick.
9. Put in the sauce boat and serve with the chicken that has been arranged in a source.

HONEY BAKED CHICKEN

ingredients

- × 3 or 4 lbs. chicken, cut up
- × 1/2 c. margarine, melted
- × 1/2 c. honey
- × 1 tsp. salt
- × 1/4 c. prep. mustard
- × 1 tsp. curry

directions

1. Pour over chicken.

2. Bake at 350 degrees for 1 1/4 hours. Basting every 15 minutes.

CORDON BLEU

ingredients

× 3 whole chicken breast, split, skinned and boned 3 slices (4 oz.) Swiss cheese, cut in half

× 3 slices (4 oz.) boiled ham, cut in half 2 tbsp. margarine

× 1 can cream of chicken soup 1/4 c. milk

× Chopped parsley

directions

1. Flatten the chicken breast.

2. Top each with 1/2 slice of cheese and then with ham.

3. Secure it with toothpicks. In a skillet, brown chicken chicken side down in margarine or butter.

4. Add the soup, milk and cover.

5. Cook over low heat for 20 minutes.

6. Stir occasionally.

7. Top with parsley.

8. For 6.

BAKED CHICKEN

ingredients

- × 1/2 c. ketchup
- × 1/2 c. mayonnaise
- × 3 tbsp. minced onion
- × Bread crumbs or crushed corn flakes
- × 2 to 2 1/2 cut up chicken

directions

1. Mix the first three ingredients and dip the chicken in it. Cover with crumbs or flakes.

2. Bake in a greased skillet or lined skillet.

3. Bake at 375 degrees for 40 to 45 minutes.

SICILIAN CHICKEN

ingredients

- × 1 tbsp. plus 1 tbsp. saffron ace 1 lg. onion, sliced
- × 1 lg. green pepper, sliced
- × 1/2 c. fresh mushberries, sliced
- × 1 1/2 lbs. boneless chicken cubed
- × 18 oz. can tomato sauce
- × 16 oz. tomatoes, chopped drained
- × 1 tsp. Worcestershire sauce
- × 1 tsp. oregano
- × 1/2 tsp. basil
- × 1/4 tsp. garlic powder
- × Lite salt and pepper to taste

directions

1. Heat oil in large nonstick skillet.
2. Add the onion, green pepper, and mushrooms.
3. Cook until slightly tender.
4. Add the chicken.
5. Cook, turning chicken frequently until pink color disappears.
6. Add the remaining ingredients.
7. Cover and simmer for 5 to 10 minutes until heated through. Serve over rice.
8. Makes 4 servings (1 protein, 2 vegetables per serving).

ROAST CHICKEN WITH ALMONDS

ingredients

- × 10 chicken breast halves Salt and pepper
- × 1 (5 1/2 oz.) pkg. slivered almonds
- × 1 (10 1/2 oz.) can cream of mushroom soup
- × 1 (10 1/2 oz.) can cream of chicken soup
- × 1/4 to 1/2 c. dry white wine, or water or other liquid Parmesan cheese

directions

1. Spread chicken in a lightly greased baking dish.
2. Cover with
3. 2/3 of the almonds.
4. Mix soups with wine.
5. Pour over the chicken and almonds.
6. Sprinkle Parmesan cheese on top and then sprinkle with the remaining almonds.
7. Bake at 350 degrees for 2 hours uncovered. Serves 8-10.

WALDORF CHICKEN

ingredients

- × 6 chicken breasts, boned and skinned 1 c. unsweetened apple juice
- × 1/4 tsp. ground ginger 1 tbsp. cornstarch
- × 2 c. unpared red apples, chopped 2 stalks celery, sliced
- × 3 tbsp. raisins
- × 1 tbsp. sliced green onion 1 tbsp. lemon juice
- × 1/4 tsp. salt, opt.
- × Ingredients: no

directions

1. Place chicken, 1/2 cup apple juice and lemon juice, salt, and pepper in a nonstick skillet.
2. Bring to a boil, cover, and simmer 20 minutes or until chicken is tender and cooked through.
3. Remove the chicken.
4. Mix in the remaining apple juice and cornstarch.
5. Stirring constantly.
6. Add the remaining ingredients. Place the chicken on a plate.
7. Top with sauce.

ORIENTAL CHICKEN

ingredients

- × 1 chicken breast, quarter, cut into slivers
- × 1/2 c. onion, sliced
- × 1/2 c. carrots, sliced
- × 1/2 c. mushrooms, sliced 1 tbsp. peanut oil
- × 1 garlic clove
- × 2 tbsp. low, sodium soy sauce

directions

1. Heat the oil in a large skillet or wok.

2. Sauté all ingredients except soy sauce over high heat.

3. Sauté for 13 minutes and lower the heat to medium and cook until the chicken is cooked through and the legs are tender and crisp about 10 minutes.

4. Mix with soy sauce.

CHICKEN YUM YUM!

ingredients

- × 1/2 pt. sour cream
- × 8 chicken breasts boned 8 slices ham
- × 1 can cream of chicken soup
- × 1 can cream of celery soup
- × 1 can cream of mushroom soup
- × 1/4 c. sherry cooking wine, opt.

directions

1. Chicken on the bone, wrap in a slice of ham.
2. Mix other ingredients together.
3. Place the chicken in a baking dish and pour the other ingredients on top.
4. Bake about 2 hours at 325 degrees.

CHICKEN IN ORANGE SAUCE

ingredients

- × 4 chicken breast halves
- × 1/4 c. flour
- × Salt and pepper
- × 4 tbsp. margarine
- × 1 1/2 c. orange juice

directions

1. Cover each half of the breast with seasoned flour.

2. Melt the margarine in a skillet and sauté each side over medium heat until lightly browned.

3. Add orange juice and cover.

4. Cook 15 to 20 more minutes over low heat until done.

5. Serve over rice, if desired, with the sauce. For 4 people.

CHICKEN AND RICE

ingredients

× 3/4 c. rice

× 2 cans cream of chicken soup

× 1 pkg. Lipton cup soup cream of chicken

× 2 c. water

× Chicken pieces, about 2 lbs.

directions

1. Mix the rice, soups, and water and put in a greased 13 x 9 saucepan.

2. Place the chicken pieces on top and cover with aluminum foil.

3. Bake at 325 degrees for 90 minutes.

4. Remove the foil and let it brown for another 15 to 20 minutes.

5. It can be prepared the day before and refrigerated until baked.

CHICKEN PILAF

ingredients

- × 1 1/3 c. Minute Rice
- × 1 envelope onion soup mix
- × 1 can cream of mushroom soup
- × 1 1/2 c. boiling water
- × 4 tbsp.
- × Melted butter Sprinkle pepper and salt 4 pieces chicken

directions

1. Combine all ingredients in an ovenproof dish. Brush the chicken with melted butter and sprinkle with salt and pepper.

2. Place on top of the casserole mixture.

3. Cover with foil and bake 1 hour and 15 minutes until chicken is cooked. It can be arranged ahead of time and then baked.

POTTED CHICKEN WITH PEPPERS AND MUSHROOMS

ingredients

- × 4 chicken breasts
- × 3 green peppers
- × 2 (3 oz.) cans mushrooms
- × 1 lg. onion
- × 4 potatoes
- × 1 tsp. salt
- × 1/2 tsp. pepper
- × 1 1/2 tsp. paprika Oil for browning
- × 1 c. water

directions

1. Brown chicken and remove from pot; brown the sliced peppers and remove from the pot.

2. Brown the onions and mushrooms together; add bell peppers and chicken, as well as seasonings and water.

3. Cover and simmer after the first boil for 2 hours.

4. Remove the chicken, it should be soft.

5. Add coarsely peeled potatoes and cook an additional 15 to 20 minutes until cooked in sauce.

MARINATED CHICKEN

ingredients

- × 1 c. soy sauce
- × 1/3 c. lemon juice
- × 1/4 c. dry sherry or wine
- × 1/4 chopped green onion
- × 1 garlic clove
- × Pinch of pepper

directions

1. Combine all ingredients in a glass or ceramic container and mix well.

2. Marinate chicken for 12 to 24 hours then either grill or broil.

3. Makes enough for 4 to 6 pieces of chicken.

CHICKEN KABOBS

ingredients

- × 3 boneless chicken breasts
- × 2 jars baby juice (Apple or peach juice) Teriyaki sauce
- × Fresh garlic crushed One clove
- × 2 jars baby food peaches

directions

1. Combine the juice, peaches, garlic, and teriyaki sauce in a 13 x 9 plate.

2. Add enough teriyaki to your liking.

3. Cut the chicken into chunks to place on a skewer.

4. Put in marinade overnight.

5. Put the chicken on the skewers.

6. Cook on the grill. While cooking, drizzle well with marinade. Serve with vegetables over rice.

RUSSIAN CHICKEN

ingredients

- × 1 pkg. dry onion soup
- × 8 oz. bottle red Russian dressing
- × 8 oz. jar apricot preserves
- × Cut up chicken

directions

1. Place chicken in baking pan.
2. Combine ingredients and pour over chicken.
3. Bake at 350 degrees for 1 hour.

TURKEY DIVAN

ingredients

- × 1 (10 oz.) pkg. frozen broccoli
- × 4 lg. slices cooked turkey or chicken
- × 1 can cream of chicken or celery soup
- × 1/3 c. milk
- × 1/4 c. Parmesan grated cheese

directions

1. Cook and drain the broccoli. Arrange in a 10 x 6 x 2 baking dish.

2. Combine sour and milk.

3. Pour over turkey.

4. Sprinkle with cheese.

5. Bake in 425 degree oven for about 15 to 20 minutes until golden brown and bubbly. 3 or 4 servings.

SCALLOPED CHICKEN

ingredients

- × 1/2 loaf white bread cubed
- × 1 1/2 c. cracker crumbs, divided 3 c. chicken broth
- × 3 eggs, lightly beaten 1 tsp. salt
- × 3/4 c. diced celery
- × 2 tbsp. chopped onion
- × 3 c. cubed cooked chicken
- × 1 can (8 oz.) sliced mushrooms, drained 1 tbsp. butter or margarine

directions

1. In a bowl, combine the bread cubes and 1 cup of the cookie crumbs.

2. Add the broth, eggs, salt, celery, onion, chicken, and mushrooms.

3. Pour into a greased 2-quart casserole. In a saucepan, melt the butter, brown the rest of the cookie crumbs.

4. Sprinkle over the casserole.

5. Bake at 350 degrees for 1 hour. Yield: 6 to 8 servings.

CHICKEN A LA KING

ingredients

- × 1/4 c. chopped onion
- × 2 tbsp. chopped green pepper
- × 2 tbsp. margarine
- × 1 can cream of chicken soup
- × 1/2 c. milk
- × 1 1/2 c.
- × Cooked, cubed, chicken or turkey
- × 2 tbsp. diced pimiento
- × Dash red pepper

directions

1. Cook the onion and green pepper in butter until tender.

2. Add the soup and milk.

3. Add the chicken and the remaining ingredients.

4. Heat and serve over toast or cooked rice. For 4 people.

APRICOT CHICKEN

ingredients

- × 3 - 4 lbs. chicken parts
- × 1 (10 oz.) jar apricot preserves
- × 1 (8 oz.) bottle Kraft Creamy French Dressing 1 pkg. Knorr's Onion Soup Mix

directions

1. Mix ingredients together and pour over chicken.

2. Bake at 350 degrees for 1 hour. Serve with rice.

BOWL OF THE WIFE OF KIT CARSON

ingredients

- × 4 c. chicken broth
- × 1 (15 oz.) can garbanzo beans, drained
- × 1 c. chicken, cubed and cooked
- × 1 - 2 chipotle peppers, minced, or 1 tsp. dried pepper flakes Dash Liquid Smoke
- × 1/2 tsp. paprika
- × 1/2 tsp. dried oregano, crushed
- × 1 med. avocado, sliced
- × 1 c. rice, cooked and hot
- × 1 c. monterey jack cheese, cubed

directions

1. Bring the broth to a boil; add beans, chicken, chili peppers, Liquid Smoke, paprika, and oregano.

2. Cover and simmer for 5 to 10 minutes.

3. Add avocado slices.

4. Place rice and cheese chunks in soup bowls.

5. Serve in hot soup. For 6.

CHICKEN A LA WORCESTERSHIRE WINE SAUCE

ingredients

- × 2 tbsp. veg. oil
- × 2 1/2 lb. chicken, cut up Salt and pepper, to taste
- × 16 baby carrots, peeled, or 2 lg. carrots, peeled and cubed
- × 1 med. red onion, sliced, or 16 pearl onions, peeled
- × 1 green bell pepper, sliced
- × 1 red bell pepper, sliced
- × 16 sm. mushrooms, sliced
- × 3/4 c. Lea and Perrins White Wine Worcestershire Sauce
- × 1/4 c. yogurt or light cream

directions

1. Heat oil in large skillet, season chicken, and brown pieces over moderately high heat until golden brown on all sides, about 15 minutes.

2. Add the vegetables and flip the glaze.

3. Drain off excess fat.

4. Pour white wine Worcestershire sauce over everything.

5. Cook 15 more minutes, basting occasionally, until chicken and vegetables are tender.

6. Add the yogurt or cream and warm. For 4 people.

BISCUIT DUMPLINGS

ingredients

- × 1/4 c. Crisco
- × 2 c. self-rising flour 1/3 c. milk

directions

1. Cut Crisco into flour then stir in milk. Drop by spoonfuls into broth.

2. Cover and simmer for 20 minutes.

CHICKEN AND BROCCOLI WITH RICE

ingredients

- × 1 1/2 c. water
- × 1 1/2 c. Minute Premium long grain rice
- × 1 lb. chicken breasts, boned and cut into strips 2 tbsp. oil
- × 1 (10 3/4 oz.) can cream of chicken soup 1/2 can milk
- × 2 tbsp. Dijon style mustard
- × 1/2 c. cheddar or Swiss cheese, grated 1 1/2 c. broccoli cuts
- × 2 tbsp. pimento, chopped (optional)

directions

1. Bring the water to a boil.

2. Add the rice.

3. Cover, remove from heat, let stand 5 minutes. Meanwhile, cook and stir chicken in hot oil until lightly browned.

4. Add the soup, milk, mustard and cheese, add the broccoli and bell pepper.

5. Bring to a boil. Reduce heat and simmer for 2 minutes.

6. Pour over the rice. For 4 people.

CHICKEN AND DUMPLINGS

ingredients

- × 1 stewing chicken, cut into pieces
- × 4 c. water
- × 3 stalks celery with leaves, cut into chunks
- × 1 carrot, peeled and sliced
- × 1/2 c. onion, coarsely chopped
- × 2 tsp. salt
- × 1/4 tsp. pepper
- × 1/3 c. flour
- × 1 c. milk
- × 2 tsp. parsley, minced Biscuit dumplings (below)

directions

1. Combine the first seven ingredients in a large covered saucepan.

2. Bring to a boil. Reduce to a simmer for 2 1/2 hours.

3. Remove the chicken to a plate. Strain the broth, measure, and add enough water to make 3 cups of liquid.

4. Mix the flour and milk. Return the broth to the skillet and bring to a boil.

5. Add the flour and milk mixture.

6. Cook until thickened, stirring constantly, and simmer 3 to 5 minutes. Return chicken pieces to sauce and cover.

7. Make meatballs. Drop spoonfuls into a gently bubbling sauce.

8. Cover the skillet and cook for 20 to 25 minutes. Before serving, sprinkle with parsley.

CHICKEN AND RICE ALMONDINE SQUASH

ingredients

- × 3 acorn squash, halved
- × 1/2 c. almonds, natural sliced
- × 1/4 c. margarine
- × 2 tbsp. maple syrup
- × 1 c. long grain rice
- × 1 c. chicken broth
- × 1/4 c. raisins
- × 2 tsp. orange peel
- × 2 chicken breasts, cubed
- × 2 tbsp. margarine Pepper
- × Garlic powder

directions

1. Bake squash at 350 degrees for 45 minutes in 1 water.

2. When squash is baked

CHICKEN BREASTS IN SOUR CREAM

ingredients

- × 6 chicken breasts, split and boned
- × 2 c. sour cream
- × 1/4 c. lemon juice
- × 2 tsp. salt
- × 4 tsp. worcestershire sauce
- × 3 tsp. garlic salt
- × 1/2 tsp. paprika
- × 1/2 tsp. pepper
- × 1 c. breadcrumbs
- × 1/2 c. margarine, melted
- × 1/2 c. butter, melted

directions

1. Rinse the chicken breasts and pat dry. In a bowl, combine sour cream, lemon juice, and seasonings.

2. Roll the chicken breasts in the sour cream mixture, place in a bowl, and top with the remaining sour cream.

3. Cover; refrigerate overnight.

4. Remove the chicken breasts, absorbing as much of the sour cream mixture as possible.

5. Roll the chicken in breadcrumbs to coat well.

6. Place in a baking dish.

7. Mix margarine and butter; Pour half of the melted butter and margarine over the chicken and bake at 350 degrees for 45 minutes.

8. Pour the remaining butter sauce over the chicken and bake 5 more minutes. For 6.

CHICKEN IN SOUR CREAM GRAVY

ingredients

- × 2 sm. fryer chickens, cut up
- Salt and pepper, to taste
- × 1/4 lb. butter or margarine
- × 3 c. milk
- × 2 tbsp. parsley, chopped
- × 1/4 c. sherry
- × 1 1/2 c. sour cream

directions

1. Season the chicken with salt and pepper.

2. Sauté in butter until golden brown.

3. Place the chicken and the fat in a saucepan.

4. Cover with milk.

5. Cook very slowly (around 325-350 degrees), around 30 minutes or until tender.

6. Add the parsley and sherry.

7. Cook for 5 to 10 more minutes.

8. Add the sour cream and stir into the sauce. Keep in the oven for another 5 minutes or more. Verify that it is ready.

CHICKEN BREASTS IN SOUR CREAM WITH MUSHROOMS

ingredients

- × 4 whole chicken breasts, halved
- × 1 (4 oz.) can sliced mushrooms, drained
- × 1 can cream of mushroom soup
- × 1/2 soup can sherry wine
- × 1 c. sour cream
- × Paprika

directions

1. Place the chicken in a shallow baking dish so the pieces do not overlap.

2. Cover with mushrooms.

3. Combine undiluted soup, sherry, and sour cream, mixing well.

4. Pour over chicken, covering completely. Sprinkle with paprika. Bake at 350 degrees for 1 1/2 hours. For 4 people.

CHICKEN BREAST WITH HONEY – WINE SAUCE

ingredients

- × 1 c. dry white wine
- × 4 tbsp. soy sauce
- × 1/4 tsp. garlic powder
- × 4 chicken breasts, skinned, boned and cut into pieces
- × 4 tbsp. veg. oil
- × 1/2 c. honey
- × 1/2 c. flour
- × 1 tsp. salt
- × 1/2 tsp. pepper

directions

1. In a large bowl, combine the wine, soy sauce, and garlic powder.

2. Add the chicken pieces, toss to coat, and marinate for 1 hour in the refrigerator.

3. Drain the chicken, reserving the marinade. On a shallow plate, mix the flour, salt, and pepper.

4. Lightly drain the chicken, one piece at a time, in the flour. In a large skillet, heat oil until moderately hot.

5. Add chicken and cook, turning, until golden brown on all sides.

6. Add honey to the reserved marinade and pour over the chicken.

7. Cover and simmer for about 15 to 20 minutes or until tender. Transfer chicken to serving platter and pour sauce over it. Serve over buttered noodles. For 4 people.

CHICKEN CASSEROLE

ingredients

- × 2 c. chicken, cooked and cut into small pieces
- × 1/4 lb. egg noodles
- × 1 can cream of chicken soup
- × 4 c. Stove Top Stuffing mix
- × 1 stick butter, melted
- × 1/2 c. milk
- × Butter 1 1/2-quart casserole dish.

directions

1. Cook the noodles according to the package, drain and pour onto a plate.

2. Top with cooked chicken and chicken soup.

3. Mix the butter with the filling mixture and put on top of the soup.

4. Pour the milk over the casserole.

5. Bake at 350 degrees for 25 minutes. Makes 4-6 servings.

CHICKEN CASSEROLE

ingredients

- × 1 (10 oz.) box Wheat Thins, crushed
- × 2 c. chicken, cooked and diced
- × 1 (15 oz.) can asparagus, cut spears
- × 1 (8 oz.) can water chestnuts, sliced
- × 2 cans cream of chicken soup
- × 1 c. Hellmann's mayonnaise
- × 1 c. cheddar cheese, grated 1 stick butter or margarine

directions

1. Combine soup and mayonnaise.

2. Place 1/2 of crushed Wheat Thins in the bottom of a 9 x 13" greased baking dish.

3. Place 1/2 of the soup and mayonnaise mixture

CHICKEN ALMOND CASSEROLE

ingredients

- × 1 c. chicken breast, diced and cooked
- × 1 can cream of chicken soup
- × 1 c. sliced almonds
- × 1/2 c. mayonnaise
- × 1 c. celery, chopped
- × 1/2 tsp. salt
- × 1/2 tsp. pepper
- × 1 tsp. lemon juice
- × 3 eggs, hard-boiled
- × 1 c. cracker crumbs (I use Zesta)
- × 2 1/2 tsp. butter

directions

1. Mix in cookie crumbs and butter; set aside.

2. Combine chicken, chicken soup, almonds, mayo, celery, salt, pepper, eggs, and lemon juice. Grease a deep casserole and pour mixed ingredients in alternate layers with 3/4 cup buttered cookie crumbs.

3. Bake at 400 degrees for 20 to 30 minutes or until bubbly.

4. Top with remaining buttered crumbs and brown. For 6.

CHICKEN CHARDONNAY

ingredients

- × 2 (6 oz.) chicken breasts, boned and skinned
- × 2 tbsp. butter
- × 2 tbsp. shallots, chopped
- × 1 c. fresh mushrooms, sliced
- × 1/4 c. chardonnay (or other dry white wine)
- × 1 tbsp. lemon juice
- × Flour
- × 1 tbsp. veg. oil
- × 1/4 c. heavy cream Parsley, chopped

directions

1. Flat chicken pound; set aside. In butter, fry the shallots; add the mushrooms and sauté for 2 to 3 minutes.

2. Add the wine and lemon juice; simmer 6 to 7 minutes.

3. Dredge chicken in flour and season if desired.

4. Sauté in oil in a frying pan.

5. Add the cream to the mushroom mixture and heat until reduced. In hot plates, place the mushrooms on the chicken breasts.

6. Sprinkle with chopped parsley and serve immediately.

CHICKEN CURRY

ingredients

- × 10 chicken drumsticks (or other cuts)
- × 3 med. potatoes
- × 4 tbsp. curry powder (or more if desired)
- × 8 oz. sour cream
- × 2 lg.
- × Cooking onions
- × 2 piece fresh ginger
- × 3 cloves garlic
- × Salt to taste
- × 5 tbsp.
- × Cooking oil
- × 1 c. water"

directions

1. Cut the cooked onions, ginger, and garlic into smaller pieces.

2. Put them in a food processor and chop finely. Peel and cut the potatoes into quarters.

3. Mix the curry powder with a little water to make a paste.

4. Heat the oil in a nonstick Dutch oven.

5. Sauté the diced onion mixture until fragrant.

6. Add the curry paste and sauté, mixing well for 2 minutes.

7. Add the chicken and potatoes.

8. Mix well.

9. Cook, covered, for about 2 minutes.

10. Add sour cream and water.

11. Mix well.

12. Bring to a boil and reduce heat to simmer.

13. Cook, covered, over low heat for about 30 minutes.

14. Curry tastes best if it's made ahead of time and served later with warm fluffy rice or thick whole wheat bread.

CHICKEN ENCHILADAS

ingredients

- × 6 chicken breasts, halved, cooked and diced
- × 1 med. onion, chopped and saut√©ed in butter
- × 8 oz. cream cheese, softened
- × 1 sm. can green chilies, chopped
- × 1 pkg. med. flour tortillas
- × 1 can cream of chicken soup
- × 3/4 c. water
- × 8 oz. sour cream
- × Cheddar cheese, shredded

directions

1. Combine chicken, onion, cream cheese, and chili peppers.

2. Spoon into the flour tortilla and roll up.

3. Place in a greased Pyrex baking dish seam side down.

4. Combine soup, water, and sour cream.

5. Pour over the tortillas.

6. Bake in preheated 350 degree oven for 35 to 40 minutes.

7. Sprinkle with cheddar cheese and heat until melted. It can be served with rice and beans. It can be frozen, but omit the cheese before freezing. Serves 8-10.

CHICKEN SHERRY

ingredients

- × 6 chicken breasts, boned
- × 3/4 c. olive oil
- × 1 stick butter or margarine
- × 1/4 bunch parsley
- × 1 onion, chopped
- × 2 c. beef consomm√©
- × 3/4 c. tomato juice
- × 1/2 c. dry sherry
- × 4 tbsp. flour

directions

1. Peel the breasts, roll them up and brown them in butter and olive oil.

2. Put the breasts in the toaster.

3. Add the flour to the oil and butter and add the remaining ingredients.

4. Cook a few minutes and pour over the chicken on the grill.

5. Cover the toaster and bake at 325-350 degrees for about 2 hours.

6. If frozen (sauce is best after freezing for a week), bake for just 1/2 hour.

7. Thaw all day when serving and bake for the remaining 1 1/2 hours at 325 degrees.

CHICKEN PECAN QUICHE

ingredients

- × 1 c. flour
- × 1 1/2 c. sharp cheddar cheese, shredded
- × 3/4 c. chopped pecans
- × 1/2 tsp. salt
- × 1/4 tsp. coarse pepper
- × 1/3 c. veg. oil
- × 3 eggs, beaten
- × 8 oz. sour cream
- × 1/4 c. mayonnaise
- × 1/2 c. chicken broth
- × 2 c. chicken, cooked and cooled
- × 1/2 c. sharp cheddar cheese, shredded
- × 1/4 c. onion, minced
- × 1/4 tsp. dillweed
- × 1/4 c. pecans, chopped

directions

1. Combine the first five ingredients.

2. Add the oil and reserve 1/4 of the mixture.

3. Put the rest in the bottom of a cake tin 9.

4. Bake 10 minutes at 350 degrees.

5. Combine the rest of the ingredients and put them on the crust.

6. Sprinkle the remaining 1/4 of the mixture on top and bake at 325 degrees for 45 minutes.

CHICKEN SARONNO

ingredients

- × 6 chicken breasts, boned, skinned and halved
- × Salt
- × Pepper
- × Garlic powder Curry powder Flour
- × 1/4 c. butter or margarine
- × 1/2 lb. fresh mushrooms, thickly sliced
- × 1/4 c. Amaretto di Saronno
- × Grated rind and juice of 1 lemon
- × 1 1/2 c. chicken broth
- × 1 tbsp. cornstarch Patty shells

directions

1. Cut chicken into 1 wide strips.
2. Sprinkle with salt

CHICKEN WELLINGTON

ingredients

- × 4 chicken breasts, boned and halved
- × 1 pkg. Uncle Ben's Wild Rice Mix
- × 1 pkg. Pillsbury crescent rolls
- × 1 egg, separated

directions

1. Cook rice according to package directions. Beat the egg white and add to the rice.

2. Pour the rice over half the chicken.

3. Cover with the other half. Separate the dough into 4 pieces, using 2 rolls for each piece.

4. Roll each piece with a rolling pin until thin.

5. Wrap a thin piece of batter around the chicken, covering completely.

6. Place the chicken on a baking sheet and brush with egg yolk.

7. Cover the pan with aluminum foil.

8. Bake at 350 degrees for 30 minutes.

9. Uncover and bake for another 20 to 30 minutes until golden brown. Serve with currant sauce (below).

10. For 4 people.

CURRANT SAUCE

ingredients

- × 1 jar red currant jelly
- × 1 tsp. worcestershire sauce
- × 1 tsp. lemon juice
- × Dash tabasco
- × 1 tsp. dry mustard

directions

1. Mix together and heat over low heat until melted.

CHUNKY CHICKEN CASSEROLE

ingredients

- × 4 chicken breasts, cooked and cut up
- × 2 cans green beans
- × 1 can water chestnuts, sliced
- × 2 cans cream of chicken soup
- × 1 c. mayonnaise
- × 2 tbsp. lemon juice Cheddar cheese, grated

directions

1. Mix together soup, mayonnaise and lemon juice. In 9 x 13" pan

CONTINENTAL CHICKEN

ingredients

- × 1 (2 1/4 oz.) pkg. dried beef, rinsed
- × 3 - 4 chicken breasts, halved and boned
- × 6 - 8 slices smoked, lean bacon
- × 1 (10 3/4 oz.) can cream of mushroom soup
- × 1/4 c. sour cream mixed with
- × 1/4 c. flour

directions

1. Place the beef jerky in the bottom of a greased slow cooker.

2. Wrap each piece of chicken with a strip of bacon and place on top of the dried meat.

3. Mix the soup, sour cream, and flour.

4. Pour over the chicken.

5. Cover and simmer 7 to 9 hours (or high for 3 to 4 hours).

6. Serve over hot buttered noodles or with rice. Makes 6 to 8 servings.

CREAMY HAM AND CHICKEN MEDLEY

ingredients

- × 1 tbsp. butter
- × 1/2 c. fresh mushrooms, sliced 1/3 c. butter
- × 1/3 c. flour
- × 2 1/2 - 3 c. milk, divided 1 c. Half & Half
- × 1 c. parmesan cheese, freshly grated 1/2 tsp. salt
- × 1/4 tsp. black pepper 1/4 tsp. nutmeg
- × 2 c. chopped cooked chicken 2 c. chopped cooked ham
- × 2 (10 oz.) pkgs. frozen puff pastry shells, baked

directions

1. Melt 1 tablespoon of butter in large saucepan over medium heat; add mushrooms and cook until tender, stirring constantly.

2. Remove from the saucepan and reserve.

3. Melt 1/3 cup butter in saucepan over low heat; add flour, stirring until smooth.

4. Cook 1 minute, stirring constantly.

5. Gradually add 2 1/2 cups of milk; cook over medium heat, stirring constantly, until thickened and bubbly.

6. Add the whipped cream and the next five ingredients.

7. Cook, stirring constantly, until cheese is melted and mixture is smooth; add the chicken and ham.

8. Add enough remaining 1/2 cup milk for a finer consistency.

9. To serve, pour in the shells. The yield of the sauce is 10 shells. Note: This can be made a day in advance and refrigerated.

10. Either in the microwave or place on the stove to warm gently. It can be served over pasta.

11. Serve with a crunchy green salad.

CHICKEN FRIED RICE

ingredients

- × 1 c. chicken, diced and cooked
- × 1 tbsp. soy sauce
- × 1 c. long grain rice, uncooked
- × 1/3 c. salad oil
- × 2 1/2 c. chicken broth
- × 2 1/2 c. onion, coarsely chopped
- × 1/4 c. green pepper, finely chopped
- × 1/4 c. celery, thinly sliced
- × 2 eggs, slightly beaten
- × 1 c. lettuce, finely shredded

directions

1. Combine the chicken, soy sauce, and 1/2 teaspoon of salt and let rest for 15 minutes.

2. Cook rice in hot oil in a skillet over medium heat until golden brown, stirring frequently. Reduce heat and add chicken with soy sauce and broth.

3. Cook over low heat, covered, for 20 to 25 minutes or until rice is tender.

4. Remove the lid for the last few minutes.

5. Add the onion, green bell pepper, and celery.

6. Cook, uncovered, over medium heat until liquid is absorbed. Push the rice mixture to the side of the pan and add the eggs.

7. Cook until almost done, then mix with the rice.

8. Add the lettuce and serve immediately.

EASY CHICKEN TETRAZZINI

ingredients

- × 1/2 pkg. fine noodles
- × 1 can mushroom soup
- × 1/4 sm. can parmesan cheese
- × 1 (4 oz.) can mushrooms, drained
- × 2 - 3 c. chicken, shredded
- × 1/2 pt. sour cream

directions

1. Boil noodles in salted water for 8 minutes.

2. Combine noodles, soup, cheese, mushrooms and chicken in a bowl.

3. Stir in sour cream.

4. Place in a greased baking dish and bake at 350 degrees for 30 minutes. Before serving, stir in a bit more cheese.

THE EYES OF TEXAS SAUSAGE CHICKEN CASSEROLE

ingredients

- × 2 c. chicken, cooked and diced
- × 1 lb. mild pork sausage
- × 1 c. celery, thinly sliced
- × 3 bunches green olives, sliced
- × 1/2 lb. fresh mushrooms, sliced (canned ones can be used)
- × 2 cloves garlic, finely minced
- × 2 cans cream of mushroom soup
- × 2 cans cream of chicken soup
- × 2 - 3 c. chicken broth
- × 1/2 c. wild rice, uncooked
- × 1 c. long grain rice, uncooked
- × 1 tbsp. worcestershire sauce (add to soup mixture)
- × 1/3 c. port wine (add to soup mixture)

directions

1. Cook long grain rice according to directions.

2. Cook wild rice about 45 minutes after washing well.

3. Drain both rices and mix.

4. Cook the sausage in a skillet until done; drain the fat.

5. Combine both soups and then add the chicken broth until you have a medium sauce.

6. Sauté the celery, garlic, onion and

7. Mushrooms until crisp-tender. In a large casserole, layer the rice, chicken, sausage, vegetables, and the soup mix.

8. Top with homemade bread croutons (see below) and bake at 350 degrees for about 45 minutes or until croutons are lightly browned and the casserole is bubbling around the edges.

FRAN'S CHICKEN

ingredients

- × 4 whole chicken breasts, skinned and boned
- × 2 cans cream of mushroom soup
- × 1 can milk
- × 16 oz. sour cream
- × 1 sm. bag Pepperidge Farm stuffing

directions

1. Prepare the filling according to the instructions on the package and let it cool.

2. Cook chicken, cut breasts in half and place in 9 x 13 "baking dish.

3. Mix soup

Anatomy of the Chicken

FRONT VIEW

DRUMSTICK

BREAST

WING →

SIDE VIEW

BACK VIEW

WING

THIGH

WING

DRUMSTICK

THIGH

ANATOMY OF THE CHICKEN

Head

The head is the talkie part of South Africa's famous walkie-talkies and stewing and braising are the best ways to cook it.

Breast

This very lean cut is best cooked quickly to keep them moist, for instance grilling, frying and braaiing. When stewing for braising breasts, don't overcook them as they will become dry and stringy.

Wing

Wings are high in fat and can withstand heat without becoming dry. They therefore are suited to deep- frying, braaiing and roasting. But however you cook them,

Tail

TAILS The tail is often attached to the thigh. It is packed with flavour because it contains a lot of fat and, thanks to the large skin area, becomes very crispy.

ANATOMY OF THE CHICKEN

Neck

This bony cut has very little meat but is an inexpensive way to flavour sauces and stock.

Thighs

Like drumsticks, thighs will be rather tough if not cooked properly. They have loads of fantastic flavour and are best when roasted or braised slowly or added to stews.

Drumstic

This popular cut could also be tough if it hasn't been cooked for long enough. The delicious dark brown meat particularly takes time and drumsticks taste best when they've been roasted, stewed, braised or braaied.

Feet

The other half of walkie-talkies, chicken feet are bony and low on meat. Once cooked, though, they are tender and can be eaten whole. Braai or grill them if you like crisp, crunchy skin.

HOW MANY CALORIES IN CHICKEN?

Chicken tenders

263 calories per 3.5 ounces (100 grams)

Back

137 calories per 3.5 ounces (100 grams)

Dark meat

125 calories per 3.5 ounces (100 grams)

Light meat

114 calories per 3.5 ounces (100 grams)

HOW MANY CALORIES IN CHICKEN?

Breast

A 3.5-ounce (100-gram) serving of chicken breast provides 165 calories, 31 grams of protein and 3.6 grams of fat.

Thigh

A 3.5-ounce (100-gram) serving of chicken thigh provides 209 calories, 26 grams of protein and 10.9 grams of fat.

Wing

Per 3.5 ounces (100 grams), chicken wings provide 203 calories, 30.5 grams of protein and 8.1 grams of fat.

Drumstick

Per 3.5 ounces (100 grams), chicken drumsticks have 172 calories, 28.3 grams of protein and 5.7 grams of fat.

Skin

While a skinless chicken breast is 284 calories with 80% protein and 20% fat, those numbers **dramatically** shift when you include the skin. One boneless, cooked chicken breast with skin (196 grams) contains: Calories: 386, Protein: 58.4 grams, Fat: 15.2 grams

COOKING METHODS

Grilling

This is one of the more common cooking methods, as it tends to require less added fat.

Baking or roasting

These other common methods are sufficient when you don't have access to a grill.

Broiling

This is similar to grilling, but you usually do it in a standard oven or toaster oven.

Braising

Lightly panfry the chicken and then cook it covered, submerged in liquid, for an extended time at a lower temperature.

COOKING METHODS

Fried

The chicken is submerged in hot cooking oil in either a pan or deep fryer. This creates a crisp outer coating but adds quite a bit of fat.

Baking or roasting

These other common methods are sufficient when you don't have access to a grill.

Boiling

You submerge the meat in boiling water and cook it until the internal temperature reaches 165°F (74°C). This is the leanest method, as it doesn't require added fats. Still, some may find the texture lacking.

Quick Recipes

Lemon Garlic Chicken

Place the whole roast chicken in the bakery with a whole lemon and a head of garlic (unpeeled) in the chicken cavity. Spice with salt and pepper. Cover with a lid and cook for 1-1 / 2 hours at 425 °. (Also try an orange).

Roasted Turkey Breast

Place the turkey breast in the bakery; Place 6-8 small red skinned potatoes, cut in half, around the turkey. Add 1/2 cup of white wine and 2 cloves of pressed garlic. Spice with salt and pepper. Cover with a lid. Bake at 350 ° F for 1-1 / 2 hours. Uncover for the last 15 to 20 minutes. Let stand 5 minutes before cutting.

Honey Mustard Chicken

Place the rotisserie chicken in the bakery and pour the fat-free honey mustard dressing on top. Cover with a lid. Roast 1-1 / 2 hours at 425 ° F.

3 CHEFS' TIPS
A little know-how can make life in the kitchen a lot easier

Done Yet

There are two ways to check if a chicken breast is done.
The first is to insert the tip of a small knife into the thickest part of the meat. If the juices run clear, it is cooked; if it's still pink,
you need to cook longer. Alternatively, make a small incision in the thickest part of the breast. If the meat is completely white and you don't see any pink meat, the brisket is done. The juices will also be clear. This method also works for testing whole chickens and other chicken pieces.

Slicing chicken breast for stir fry

Place the chicken breast, smooth side down, on a cutting board.
Cut diagonally into 1cm strips and cut each strip lengthwise in half into longer, thinner strips before cutting diagonally across the fibers to keep them tender.

Butterflying chicken breasts for schnitzels

Place the chicken breast smooth side down on a cutting board. Make a shallow incision along one side and continue as if you were trying to cut the breast into two identical halves. Stop just before cutting it all the way through, so the top and bottom half open like a book. With a meat mallet, tap the thickest part gently until it is finer and more uniform. Butterfly breasts can also be stuffed with any filling you like.

TIPS AND TRICKS

Keeping it Clean

- × Once chicken has been defrosted, do not refreeze it.
- × Don't let raw chicken come into contact with other food, cooked or un-cooked.
- × Always wash your hands, utensils and surfaces that have been in contact with raw chicken with hot, soapy water.
- × Keep a separate chopping board for raw meat to prevent cross-contamination.
- × Always make sure that meat is cooked through to kill all harmful bacteria that may have been lurking in it.

When buying chicken

Always look for chicken that has an even colour with no blemishes or bruises. The meat should look moist and plump and have a neutral smell. Check that the packaging hasn't been damaged in any way. When buying frozen chicken, make sure that the meat is frozen solid and does not have any soft areas where it has begun to defrost – and do remember to check the sell-by-date too.

Storing Chicken

Always refrigerate or freeze chicken as soon as possible after buying it. If the packet is damaged or soggy and you are going to cook it within two days, remove the chicken, pat it dry with kitchen paper and place on a plate. Cover with clingwrap or foil and put the plate on the bottom rack of the fridge. That way, it won't contaminate other food if it drips. If you want to freeze the chicken at home, remove it from the packet, pat it dry and reseal in an airtight bag.

TIPS AND TRICKS

Stop Breast Drying

How to stop the breast from drying out when MAKING roast chicken.
Roast the chicken breast-side down for two thirds of the cooking time. This way, all the juices will run down into the breast meat and keep it moist. Once you are ready to crisp the skin, carefully turn the chicken breast-side up and roast until golden.

How Tos and Hacks

Chicken salad. Place chicken breast side up on cutting board. Pull the
the leg and thigh away from the body and use your fingers to find the hip joint in the crease. Insert the tip of a large knife into the joint and cut through the skin, meat, and joint to separate the thigh and leg from the body. Repeat on the other side. Use the same method to separate the leg from the thigh and cut the wings from the body. To remove the chicken breast, cut the breast to divide the carcass in two. Cut all the bone and cartilage from the breasts.
You will now have two of each: thighs, drumsticks, wings, and breasts. Add the carcass to soups, stews or casseroles for flavor and remove the bones just before serving.

How to defrost a whole chicken

Thawing a frozen chicken is best done overnight in the fridge. Place it in a large bowl or on a plate to prevent the juices from dripping in the fridge. Before cooking it, check inside the cavity to see that there is no more ice. If pressed for time, put the bird in a bucket of cold water in the sink, but be sure to keep the water cold to prevent bacteria from growing.

TIPS AND TRICKS

Getting a golden skin

Check that the skin is completely dry, rub the whole bird generously with oil and season well.
Uncover the chicken 20-30 minutes before the end of the cooking time and place it on a shallow baking tray or on an oven rack on a tray to allow the dry heat to come into contact with as much skin as possible. Roast until the skin is crisp and glassy

Chicken and food poisoning

Raw chicken may contain natural bacteria, which could be dangerous if it hasn't been stored properly. Salmonella and campylobacter, which are linked to food poisoning and gastro, are among the most common.

3 DIPS FOR CHICKEN NUGGETS

Garlic and lemon mayo

Stir 2 finely chopped garlic cloves and zest and juice of 1/2 lemon into 1 cup (250 ml) Mayonnaise.

Tomato relish

Finely chop 3 small sherkins and 3 pickeled onions and stir into 3/4 cup (180ml) tomato sauce.

Sweet and sour

Stir together 3/4 cup (180 ml) pineapple juice, 1/4 cup (60 ml) apple cider vinegar, 1/4 cup (60 ml) brown sugar, 2 tbsp (30 ml) tomato cauce and 1 tbps (15 ml) cornflour. Thicker over a low heat.

Quick Recipes

Chicken Pot Pie

Simmer a couple of boneless, skinless chicken breasts, let cool and cube. Microwave cubed potatoes, carrots, celery, onion, green beans or peas. Combine with cornstarch-thickened chicken broth (from the simmered chicken), and pour into pie crust lined baker (you can use Pillsbury ready made) then top with the other crust, crimp, brush with milk, sprinkle with herbs, sesame seeds, or a little Parmesan, and bake at 350° about 40 min.

Cranberry Chicken

Mix one can of whole berry cranberries w/ can of cream of mushroom soup and one packet of onion soup mix. Pour over top of chicken in baker. Cover with lid, place in oven; bake for 1-1/2 hours at 425.

Chicken and Vegetables

Place chicken (skin on or off) in baker. Place chopped onion, celery and carrots around chicken. Sprinkle with 1/2 package of Good Seasons Italian Dressing mix. Place lid on top. Bake at 350° for 1 hour.

The Chicken Cookbook

Chicken Akademy

Table of Contents

TABLE OF CONTENTS	5
CHICKEN CHOPSTICK	9
FRAN'S CHICKEN	10
LEMON CHICKEN SAUTE	11
GREEK LEMON CHICKEN	12
GRILLED CHICKEN WITH FLORIDA BARBEQUE SAUCE	13
MARINATED CHICKEN BREASTS	14
MOCK CHICKEN KIEV	15
LUNCHEON CHICKEN CASSEROLE	16
RALPH AND RADINE'S FAVORITE CHICKEN SPAGHETTI	17
OVERNIGHT CHICKEN DIVAN	18
GREAT AND EASY CHICKEN CASSEROLE	19
PIZZA CHICKEN ROLL-UPS	20
HONEY-DIJON CHICKEN SALAD	21
MEDITERRANEAN CHICKEN	22
GARLIC CLOVE CHICKEN	23
CACCIATORE CHICKEN BREASTS	24
RED PEPPER CHICKEN	25
CHICKEN OLE FOIL SUPPER	26
FETA CHICKEN SALAD	27
HONEY BALSAMIC CHICKEN	28
MEDITERRANEAN CHICKEN TRAYBAKE	29
HEALTHY MISO CHICKEN SOUP	30
CITRUS-ROASTED CHICKEN RECIPE	31
STUFFED CHICKEN WITH PARMA HAM RECIPE	32
CARIBBEAN CHICKEN CURRY RECIPE	33
SPANISH CHICKEN WITH BEANS RECIPE	34
LEMON CHICKEN TRAY BAKE RECIPE	35
HONEY ROAST CHICKEN THIGHS WITH QUINOA RECIPE	36

MELLOW-SPICED CHICKEN AND CHICKPEAS RECIPE	37
APPLE CHICKEN STEW	38
BUTTER CHICKEN MURG MAKHANI RECIPE	39
SOUTHERN-FRIED CHICKEN RECIPE	40
MANGO CHUTNEY CHICKEN CURRY	41
CHILLI CHICKEN RECIPE	42
SIMPLE FRIED CHICKEN BREAST CUTLETS	43
BAKED CHICKEN WITH BACON AND PEPPER JACK CHEESE	44
PAPRIKA CHICKEN WITH SOUR CREAM GRAVY	45
EASY SKILLET CHICKEN WITH VELOUTE SAUCE	46
SIMPLE OVEN-FRIED CHICKEN BREASTS WITH GARLIC	47
SKILLET CHICKEN WITH BACON AND SOUR CREAM	48
RHONDA'S MARINATED CHICKEN SAUCE	49
CHICKEN BREASTS WITH CREAMY PARMESAN SAUCE	50
TARRAGON CHICKEN SALAD	51
OVEN-ROASTED CHICKEN WITH PEPPER JELLY GLAZE	52
AIR FRYER CHICKEN TENDERS	53
INSTANT POT CHICKEN BREAST	54
PEACH GLAZED CHICKEN BREASTS	55
CHICKEN TERIYAKI THIGHS RECIPE	56
WINE CHICKEN	57
CHICKEN POT PIE	58
MOZZARELLA CHICKEN	59
BAKED CHICKEN PARMESAN	60
CHICKEN AND ZUCCHINI WITH GARLIC CREAM SAUCE	61
CHICKEN WITH LEMON AND SPICY SPRING ONIONS	62
CHICKEN - BROCCOLI CASSEROLE	63
BAKED CHICKEN SALAD	64
BARBECUE CHICKEN	65
CHICKEN TURNOVERS	66
CAJUN TURKEY BURGERS	67
BRANDIED CHICKEN BREAST	68
CAROLYN'S CHICKEN & RICE	69
CHICKEN CASSOULET	70

ANATOMY OF THE CHICKEN   **74**

HOW MANY CALORIES IN CHICKEN?   **76**

COOKING METHODS   **78**

QUICK RECIPES   **80**

3 CHEFS' TIPS   **81**

TIPS AND TRICKS   **85**

3 DIPS FOR CHICKEN NUGGETS   **86**

QUICK RECIPES   **87**

Recipes

CHICKEN CHOPSTICK

ingredients

- × 2 (10 1/2 oz.) cans cream of mushroom soup
- × 1 (3 oz.) can chow mein noodles
- × 1 can or bag cashew nuts
- × 2 c. diced chicken
- × 1/2 c. water
- × 1 1/4 c. celery, cut up
- × 1/4 c. chopped onion Dash pepper

directions

1. Combine water and soup; mixture. Reserve 1/2 of the noodles for the top of the casserole.

2. Add other noodles to the soup mix with celery, walnuts, onion, and chicken and stir lightly.

3. Put the reserve noodles on top.

4. Bake for 20 to 25 minutes in 375 degree oven.

FRAN'S CHICKEN

ingredients

- × 4 whole chicken breasts, skinned and boned
- × 2 cans cream of mushroom soup
- × 1 can milk
- × 16 oz. sour cream
- × 1 sm. bag Pepperidge Farm stuffing

directions

1. Prepare stuffing according to package directions and let cool.

2. Cook chicken, cut breasts in half and lay in 9 x 13" baking dish.

3. Mix soup

LEMON CHICKEN SAUTE

ingredients

- × 6 chicken breast halves, boned and skinned
- × 3 tbsp. all-purpose flour
- × Non-stick cooking spray
- × 1/4 c. margarine
- × 1/3 c. teriyaki sauce
- × 3 tbsp. lemon juice
- × 1 tsp. fresh garlic, minced
- × 1/2 tsp. sugar
- × Rice, cooked

directions

1. Roll chicken in flour to coat.
2. Spray 10 skillet with nonstick spray.
3. Add the margarine and melt.
4. Add the chicken breasts.
5. Cook over medium heat until chicken is lightly browned.

GREEK LEMON CHICKEN

ingredients

- × MARINADE
- × 1 c. fruity white wine 1/4 c. olive oil
- × 1/4 c. fresh lemon juice
- × 1 tsp. lemon peel, freshly grated 1 tsp. salt
- × 1 tsp. freshly ground black pepper 3 cloves garlic, crushed
- × CHICKEN
- × 6 whole lg. chicken breasts, boned and skinned 3 tbsp. olive oil
- × 2 tbsp. butter
- × 2 tbsp. all-purpose flour 1/2 tsp. salt
- × 2 tsp. prepared mustard 1 c. milk
- × 2 egg yolks
- × Freshly grated peel of 1 lemon 1 tsp. fresh lemon juice
- × 1 tsp. dried dillweed
- × 1/4 c. fresh parsley, minced 1 c. sour cream
- × 1/4 c. butter, melted
- × 1/2 c. feta cheese, crumbled
- × 1 lb. angel hair pasta, cooked al dente and kept warm 1/2 c. muenster cheese, shredded

directions

1. In a bowl, combine all the marinade ingredients.

2. Lightly pound the chicken breasts and place in a shallow saucepan or Ziploc plastic bags and cover with the marinade. Refrigerate for up to 12 hours. Discard the marinade.

3. Heat oil in a skillet and sauté chicken until tender.

4. Cut and reserve. In a saucepan, melt 2 tablespoons of butter; Mix together the flour and salt to create a roux.

5. Add the mustard and slowly add the milk, stirring constantly until thick and smooth. In a small bowl, whisk together the egg yolk, lemon zest, and lemon juice.

6. Beat a small amount of roux into the egg mixture.

7. Next, mix the egg mixture into roux and bring it to a gentle boil.

8. Remove from the heat and add the dill and parsley. When the parsley wilts, add the sour cream.

9. Add 1/4 cup butter, 3/4 cup egg sauce and feta cheese to cooked pasta; stir well.

10. Place in greased 9 x 13 "casserole and top with chicken slices

GRILLED CHICKEN WITH FLORIDA BARBEQUE SAUCE

ingredients

- × Chicken for grilling
- × 2 sticks butter
- × 1/2 c. cider vinegar
- × 1/2 c. ketchup
- × 2 bottles prepared horseradish (9 oz.)
- × Juice of 3 lemons, or 1 c. lemon juice
- × 1/2 tsp. salt
- × 1/2 tbsp. worcestershire sauce
- × 1 tsp. hot pepper sauce (optional)

directions

1. In a stainless steel pot, melt the butter slowly.

2. Add vinegar, tomato sauce, horseradish, lemon juice, salt, Worcestershire sauce, and pepper sauce. Simmer, uncovered, for 20 to 25 minutes to blend flavors.

3. Use it as a sauce to drizzle the chicken. The sauce can be frozen.

MARINATED CHICKEN BREASTS

ingredients

- × 6 very sm. whole chicken breasts, boned, or 3 lg. ones cut in half
- × 3 med. cloves garlic, crushed
- × 1 1/2 tsp. salt
- × 1/2 c.
- × Brown sugar, packed
- × 3 tbsp. grainy mustard
- × 1/4 c. cider vinegar Juice of 1 lime
- × Juice of 1/2 lg. lemon
- × 6 tbsp. olive oil
- × Black pepper to taste

directions

1. Place the chicken breasts in a shallow bowl.

2. Mix together the garlic, salt, sugar, mustard, vinegar, and lime and lemon juices.

3. Mix well. Add the olive oil and add the pepper.

4. Pour over chicken and refrigerate overnight, covered. Rotation.

5. Remove from refrigerator 1 hour before you want to cook and allow to come to room temperature. Grill about 4 minutes per side or until done.

MOCK CHICKEN KIEV

ingredients

- × 2 whole chicken breasts, skinned, boned and halved
- × 1/2 c. dry breadcrumbs
- × 1/3 c. parmesan cheese
- × 2 tbsp. parsley, minced
- × 1 tsp. salt
- × Dash pepper
- × 1 clove garlic, minced
- × 1 lemon
- × Dash paprika
- × 1/2 c. butter or margarine

directions

1. Blend the crumbs, cheese, parsley, salt, and pepper.

2. Melt the butter and add the garlic. Lightly pound the chicken if necessary.

3. Dip the chicken in garlic butter and then the crumbs. Cover well.

4. Roll the chicken into a light roll, secure with a toothpick.

5. Place in a baking dish. Squeeze the lemon juice on top. Drizzle in the remaining butter.

6. Bake at 350 degrees for 1 hour.

LUNCHEON CHICKEN CASSEROLE

ingredients

- × 1 1/2 c. chicken, cooked and cut in bite size pieces
- × 1 c. celery, chopped
- × 2 tbsp. onions, minced
- × 3/4 c. mayonnaise
- × 1 1/2 c. rice, cooked
- × 1 can cream of chicken soup
- × 1 c. Special K cereal (or cornflakes, crushed)
- × 1/4 c. almonds
- × 2 tbsp. margarine, melted

directions

1. Cook rice as directed on box.
2. To drain.
3. Combine celery, onion, chicken, rice, mayo, and soup in 2-quart baking dish.
4. Mix well.
5. Mix margarine, almonds and Special K.
6. Cover the chicken mixture.
7. Bake, uncovered, at 325 degrees for 30 to 40 minutes.

RALPH AND RADINE'S FAVORITE CHICKEN SPAGHETTI

ingredients

- × 1 med. chicken, cooked and boned
- × 1 tbsp. margarine
- × 1/2 lg. green pepper, chopped
- × 1 med onion
- × 1/2 lb. fresh mushrooms, sliced, or 1(4 oz.) can mushrooms,
- × sliced 2 cans cream of mushroom soup or cream of chicken soup
- × 2 cans cream of tomato soup
- × 1 can chicken broth
- × 1 (7 oz.) jar green olives, drained
- × 2 tsp. worcestershire sauce
- × 3 drops tabasco sauce
- × 1 tsp. salt
- × 1/4 tsp. pepper
- × 2 (7 oz.) pkgs. spaghetti
- × 5 oz. sharp cheddar cheese, grated

directions

1. Cook spaghetti according to package directions.

2. Melt the margarine in a large skillet and add the green bell pepper, onion, and mushrooms. Saute until tender.

3. Add the soups, broth, olives, Worcestershire sauce, and Tabasco. Simmer for 15 minutes, then add the chicken, drained spaghetti, and salt and pepper.

4. Remove from heat and add 3/4 of the cheese. DO NOT cook after adding cheese.

5. Use the remaining cheese by sprinkling it over the spaghetti after pouring it into a serving plate.

OVERNIGHT CHICKEN DIVAN

ingredients

- × 8 chicken breast halves, or
- × 2 lbs. chicken tenders
- × 1 - 2 heads fresh broccoli
- × 1 can light cream of chicken soup, undiluted
- × 1/2 c. fat-free sour cream
- × 1/2 c. light mayonnaise
- × 2 tbsp. dry sherry
- × 1 tsp. paprika
- × 1 tsp. prepared mustard
- × 1/4 tsp. curry powder
- × 1/3 c. parmesan cheese, grated

directions

1. Cook the chicken, preferably sautéing it in a tablespoon of oil. Coarsely chop the meat and reserve.

2. Cook the broccoli until crisp and tender. Place broccoli in lightly greased 9 x 13 "x 2" baking dish.

3. Combine the soup and the next six ingredients (dilute if necessary with skim milk); pour half of the sauce over the broccoli. Spoon chicken over sauce; top with the remaining sauce.

4. Cover and refrigerate for up to 24 hours.

5. To bake

GREAT AND EASY CHICKEN CASSEROLE

ingredients

- × 2 lg. chicken breasts, halved
- × 1 tbsp. margarine
- × 1 can cream of chicken soup
- × 3/4 c.
- × Sauterne wine
- × 1 (5 oz.) can water chestnuts, sliced
- × 1 (3 oz.) can mushrooms
- × 1/4 c. green pepper, chopped

directions

1. Fry the chicken in margarine until golden.

2. Remove to a baking dish.

3. Combine the rest of the ingredients and heat in a skillet for 5 minutes over low heat.

4. Pour the sauce over the chicken and cover with aluminum foil.

5. Bake at 350 degrees for 25 minutes. Uncover and continue cooking for another 25 minutes.

PIZZA CHICKEN ROLL-UPS

ingredients

×   4 boneless skinless chicken breast halves (4 ounces each)

×   12 pepperoni slices

×   8 slices part-skim mozzarella cheese

×   1 can (15 ounces) pizza sauce

directions

1. Flatten chicken to 1/4 inch. thickness. Place three pepperoni slices and one cheese slice on each. Roll up tightly; Secure with toothpicks. Place in greased 11x7-inch container. Baking dish. Top with pizza sauce.

2. Cover and bake at 350 ° for 35-40 minutes or until chicken is no longer pink. To find out; top with the remaining cheese. Bake for 5 more minutes or until cheese is melted. If desired, grill for a minute or two to lightly brown the cheese.

HONEY-DIJON CHICKEN SALAD

ingredients

- × 1/2 pound chicken tender-loins, cut into 1-1/2-inch pieces
- × 2 tablespoons honey, divided
- × 2 tablespoons Dijon mustard, divided
- × 3 cups torn leaf lettuce
- × 2 hard-boiled large eggs, chopped
- × 2 tablespoons each chopped green, sweet orange and yellow pepper
- × 1 tablespoon chopped onion
- × 2 teaspoons sesame seeds

directions

1. Preheat the oven to 350 °. Place chicken in greased 1-1 / 2 qt. Container. Baking dish. Combine 1 tablespoon of honey and mustard; pour over chicken. Cover and bake until chicken is no longer pink, 20-25 minutes.

2. In a large bowl, combine the lettuce, eggs, bell peppers, onion, and sesame seeds; divide between 2 plates. Top with chicken. Combine remaining tablespoon of honey and mustard; drizzle over chicken.

MEDITERRANEAN CHICKEN

ingredients

- × 4 boneless skinless chicken breast halves (6 ounces each)
- × 1/4 teaspoon salt
- × 1/4 teaspoon pepper
- × 3 tablespoons olive oil
- × 1 pint grape tomatoes
- × 16 pitted Greek or ripe olives, sliced
- × 3 tablespoons capers, drained

directions

1. Sprinkle the chicken with salt and pepper. In a large ovenproof skillet, cook chicken in oil over medium heat until golden brown, 2-3 minutes on each side. Add the tomatoes, olives, and capers.

2. Bake, uncovered, at 475° until a thermometer reads 170°, 10-14 minutes.

GARLIC CLOVE CHICKEN

ingredients

- × 1 roasting chicken (5 to 6 pounds)
- × 1 small onion, quartered
- × 40 garlic cloves, peeled
- × 1/4 cup canola oil
- × 1-1/2 teaspoons salt
- × 1 teaspoon dried parsley flakes
- × 1/2 teaspoon dried celery flakes
- × 1/2 teaspoon each dried tarragon, thyme and rosemary, crushed
- × 1/4 teaspoon pepper

directions

1. Place chicken breast side up on wire rack in shallow roasting pan. Fill the chicken with onion; tie the drumsticks together. Place the garlic cloves around the chicken. In a small bowl, combine the remaining ingredients. Drizzle the chicken and garlic.

2. Cover and bake at 350 ° for 1-3 / 4 hours. To find out; bake for an additional 30-45 minutes or until a thermometer inserted in the thickest part of the thigh reads 170 ° -175 °, drizzling occasionally with the fat from the pan. (Cover lightly with foil if chicken is browning too quickly.) Cover and let rest for 10 minutes before cutting.

CACCIATORE CHICKEN BREASTS

ingredients

- × 1/2 medium onion, sliced and separated into rings
- × 1/2 medium green pepper, sliced
- × 1 tablespoon olive oil
- × 2 boneless skinless chicken breast halves (5 ounces each)
- × 3/4 cup canned stewed tomatoes
- × 2 tablespoons white wine or chicken broth
- × 1/4 teaspoon garlic salt
- × 1/4 teaspoon dried rosemary, crushed
- × 1/8 teaspoon pepper

directions

1. In a large skillet, sauté onion and green bell pepper in oil until crisp-tender.

2. Remove and keep warm. Cook chicken over medium-high heat until juices run clear, 4-5 minutes on each side.

3. Remove and reserve.

4. Add the tomatoes, wine, garlic salt, rosemary, and pepper to the skillet.

5. Add the onion mixture and heat.

6. Serve with chicken.

RED PEPPER CHICKEN

ingredients

× 4 boneless skinless chicken breast halves (4 ounces each)

× 1 can (15 ounces) no-salt-added black beans, rinsed and drained

× 1 can (14-1/2 ounces) Mexican stewed tomatoes, undrained

× 1 jar (12 ounces) roasted sweet red peppers, drained and cut into strips

× 1 large onion, chopped

× Pepper to taste

× Hot cooked rice

directions

1. Place chicken in 3-quart container. Slow cooking pot. In a bowl, combine the beans, tomatoes, red bell peppers, onion, and bell pepper.

2. Pour over the chicken.

3. Cover and simmer until chicken is tender, about 6 hours. Serve with rice.

CHICKEN OLE FOIL SUPPER

ingredients

× 1 can (15 ounces) black beans, rinsed and drained

× 2 cups fresh or frozen corn (about 10 ounces), thawed

× 1 cup salsa

× 4 boneless skinless chicken breast halves (4 ounces each)

× 1/4 teaspoon garlic powder

× 1/4 teaspoon pepper

× 1/8 teaspoon salt

× 1 cup shredded cheddar cheese

× 2 green onions, chopped

directions

1. Mix beans, corn, and salsa; divide by four 18x12 inches. pieces of sturdy aluminum foil. Top with chicken. Mix seasonings; sprinkle over chicken. Fold the foil over the chicken, sealing tightly.

2. Grill the packages, covered, over medium heat until a thermometer inserted into the chicken reads 165 °, 15-20 minutes. Open the foil carefully to allow steam to escape. Sprinkle with cheese and chives.

FETA CHICKEN SALAD

ingredients

- × 2 cups shredded cooked chicken breasts
- × 1/2 cup cherry tomatoes, halved
- × 1/2 cup finely chopped red onion
- × 1/2 cup chopped seedless cucumber
- × 1/2 cup chopped sweet yellow pepper
- × 4 teaspoons lemon juice
- × 4 teaspoons olive oil
- × 1/2 teaspoon Greek seasoning
- × 1/2 teaspoon salt
- × 1/8 teaspoon pepper
- × 1/4 cup crumbled feta cheese

directions

1. In a large bowl, combine the first 5 ingredients. In a small bowl, whisk the lemon juice, oil, Greek seasoning, salt and pepper.

2. Pour over chicken mixture; toss to coat.

3. Refrigerate for at least 1 hour.

4. Just before serving, sprinkle with cheese.

HONEY BALSAMIC CHICKEN

ingredients

- × 2 boneless skinless chicken breast halves (5 ounces each)
- × 1/2 teaspoon garlic salt
- × 1/8 teaspoon coarsely ground pepper
- × 2 teaspoons canola oil
- × 1 tablespoon balsamic vinegar
- × 1 tablespoon honey
- × 1/2 teaspoon dried basil

directions

1. Sprinkle the chicken with garlic salt and pepper. In a large skillet over medium heat, cook chicken in oil until juices run clear, 4 to 7 minutes on each side. Remove and keep warm.

2. Add vinegar, honey, and basil to skillet; cook and stir 1 minute. Return chicken to skillet; hot, turning to coat with frosting.

MEDITERRANEAN CHICKEN TRAYBAKE

ingredients

- × Charlotte potatoes 750g, halved lengthways
- × olive oil
- × red onion 1, cut into wedges
- × garlic 1 bulb, cloves separated
- × lemon 1, cut into wedges
- × whole chicken thighs 8
- × baby plum tomatoes 12, halved
- × white wine a small glass
- × mixed olives (green and Kalamata) a handful of each
- × feta 100g, sliced
- × oregano a handful of leaves

directions

1. Heat the oven to 200C / fan 180C / gas 6. Place the potatoes on a large roasting pan, add 2 tablespoons of olive oil and season. Toss everything to coat and then roast for 20 minutes.

2. Add the red onion, garlic cloves, lemon wedges, and chicken thighs, then drizzle with another tablespoon of oil and season. Roast for another 20 minutes, then remove and turn on the oven to 220C / 200C fan / gas 7.

3. Add the tomatoes, wine and olives, then return the tray to the oven and cook for the last 20 minutes until the chicken is crispy. and gold. Sprinkle over the feta cheese and oregano, drizzle with a little more olive oil, and serve.

HEALTHY MISO CHICKEN SOUP

ingredients

- × toasted sesame oil 3 tsp
- × ginger a thumb-sized piece, finely grated
- × garlic 2 cloves, crushed
- × chicken stock 750ml
- × pak choi 1, quartered
- × mangetout 100g
- × ready-cooked udon noodles 150g pack
- × cooked chicken thighs 2
- × white miso 1 tbsp
- × gochujang 1 tbsp
- × sesame seeds 1 tbsp, toasted to serve
- × coriander a handful of leaves, chopped

directions

1. Heat 1 teaspoon of sesame oil in a large skillet and cook the ginger and garlic for a few minutes. Pour in the chicken broth, simmer, and add the pak choi, mangetout, and udon noodles, and simmer 2-3 minutes or until cooked.

2. Heat the remaining sesame oil in a nonstick skillet and shred the chicken meat, discarding the bones and skin. Fry for 2-3 minutes or until crisp, then add the miso and gochujang, and fry for one more minute.

3. Divide the veggies, noodles, and broth into 2 bowls, then top with the chicken, sesame seeds, and cilantro.

CITRUS-ROASTED CHICKEN RECIPE

ingredients

- × 4 tbsp marmalade (preferably clementine marmalade)
- × 2 tbsp olive oil
- × 1 tbsp Dijon mustard
- × 1 clove garlic, peeled and crushed
- × 1 level tbsp freshly grated ginger
- × Salt and freshly ground black pepper
- × 8-12 chicken thighs and/or drumsticks
- × 4-6 clementines, or tangerines
- × 1-2 tbsp chopped fresh parsley

directions

1. To make this chicken thigh recipe, preheat the oven to 200 ° C / 400 ° F / Gas Mark 6.

2. In a large bowl, combine the jam, olive oil, mustard, garlic, ginger, and seasoning.

3. Cut the chicken skin diagonally 3 times on each thigh / thigh. Add the chicken to the bowl and cover with the jam mixture.

4. Spread the chicken pieces out in a large roasting pan and pour over the jam juice in the bowl.

5. Thinly slice the clementines or tangerines and place them on the chicken pieces, pressing a little between the pieces.

6. Cover the roasting pan with aluminum foil and place in the center of the oven.

7. Bake for 20 minutes, then remove foil and bake for an additional 30-40 minutes, basting occasionally, until chicken begins to brown and juices run clear when meat is pierced. Remove from the oven and sprinkle with parsley before serving.

STUFFED CHICKEN WITH PARMA HAM RECIPE

ingredients

- × 4 x 125g (4 1/2 oz) boneless chicken breasts, skinned
- × 3tbsp pesto
- × 4 sun-dried tomatoes, drained of oil and sliced
- × 8 thin slices Parma ham
- × 1tbsp olive oil

directions

1. To make this chicken breast recipe, preheat the oven to 400 ° F (200 ° C, gas mark 6). Next, spread the chicken breasts out on a board and, using a sharp knife, make a small cut across the top of each to create a "pocket."

2. Spread the inside of the pocket with the classic pesto and place the dried tomato slices on each chicken breast.

3. Wrap two slices of Parma ham around each chicken breast and place on a baking sheet.

4. Finally, drizzle each one with oil and bake in the oven for 20-25 minutes or until the chicken is cooked through.

CARIBBEAN CHICKEN CURRY RECIPE

ingredients

- × 4 skinless chicken breasts, cut into 2cm (1in) cubes
- × 1tbsp oil
- × 1 small onion, peeled and finely chopped
- × 1 garlic clove, peeled
- × 5cm (2in) piece of root ginger, peeled and roughly chopped
- × 1 red chilli, deseeded
- × 1tbsp of mild curry paste
- × 400ml (14fl oz) can of coconut milk
- × 1 large mango, peeled and cut into chunks
- × 2tbsp fresh coriander, finely chopped
- × Rice and peas
- × 350g (12oz) long grain rice
- × 130g (5oz) can kidney beans, drained and rinsed
- × 2 spring onions, sliced

directions

1. To make this chicken curry, heat the oil in a medium saucepan over medium heat and add the onion, garlic, ginger, and chilli. Cook for 3-4 minutes.

2. Add chicken and cook 5 minutes, or until sealed and lightly browned.

3. Add the curry paste and cook for 1 min, add 3/4 of the coconut milk and cook over moderate heat for 20 minutes.

4. Add the mango and cilantro and simmer for 5 more minutes.

5. While the curry is cooking, prepare the rice and peas. Cook rice according to package directions. Then, 5 minutes before the end of cooking, add the coconut milk and kidney beans.

6. Drain and pile the rice into individual plates, garnish with the scallions and top with the Caribbean chicken curry.

SPANISH CHICKEN WITH BEANS RECIPE

ingredients

- × 600g chicken thighs
- × 125g skinned and sliced chorizo
- × 1 onion, peeled and sliced
- × 1tbsp olive oil
- × 1 red pepper
- × 1 large garlic clove, peeled and chopped
- × 1tbsp red pesto (or sun-dried tomato paste)
- × 410g can of cannellini beans, drained and rinsed
- × 300ml hot chicken stock
- × A few thyme sprigs
- × 1tsp smoked paprika

directions

1. To make this chicken thigh recipe, heat olive oil in a deep skillet. Add the chicken thighs skin side down, chorizo and onion skinless and sliced. Cook the chicken for 5 minutes without turning so that the skin browns, but stir in the onion and chorizo.

2. Flip the chicken and add the red bell pepper, seeded and cut into chunks, a large garlic clove, peeled and minced, red pesto (or sun-dried tomato paste), cannellini beans, drained and rinsed, chicken broth hot and a little thyme. twigs.

3. Sprinkle smoked paprika over chicken. Bring to a boil, cover, and simmer 25 minutes, until chicken is tender.

LEMON CHICKEN TRAY BAKE RECIPE

ingredients

- × For the
- × marinade:
- × 8
- × , boneless and skin on
- × 4tbsp soy sauce
- × Juice and zest of 1 lemon
- × 1tbsp sugar
- × For the
- × lemon chicken tray bake:
- × 1 onion, finely diced
- × 2 cloves garlic, crushed
- × 1tbs rosemary, very finely chopped
- × 50g breadcrumbs.
- × 400g maris piper potatoes
- × 2 red onions, quartered
- × Squeezed lemon halves from 1 lemon (keep the juice)
- × 1 head garlic, halved horizontally
- × Black pepper, to season
- × Drizzle of olive oil
- × Flat leaf parsley, to serve
- × You'll also need:
- × A roasting tray

directions

1. In a large bowl, marinate the chicken thighs in the soy sauce, juice and zest of 1 lemon and sugar for at least 2 hours.

2. Preheat oven to 200 ° C / 400 ° F fan / Gas brand 6.

3. In a large skillet, heat a little oil over medium heat and sauté the chopped onion and garlic for about 5 min until they soften, then add the rosemary and breadcrumbs.

4. Remove chicken from marinade and shake off excess, reserve marinade for drizzling. Open the thighs with a sharp knife and fill with the breadcrumb filling, use a toothpick to secure them.

5. Bring a large pot of water to a boil and boil the potatoes for 5 minutes, then drain and add them to a roasting pan along with the chicken, red onions, the squeezed lemon halves and the garlic head cut in half and then season with black pepper. .

6. Drizzle in some olive oil and bake in the preheated oven for 1 hour, 20 minutes.

7. Before the end of cooking, spread over the remaining breadcrumbs and return to the oven until golden brown.

8. Garnish with a little flat-leaf parsley and squeeze over the juice of the toasted lemons and serve.

HONEY ROAST CHICKEN THIGHS WITH QUINOA RECIPE

ingredients

- × 8 chicken thighs (skin on)
- × 1tbsp lemon juice
- × 2tbsp runny honey
- × 1tsp dried rosemary
- × Salt and freshly ground black pepper
- × 150g quinoa
- × 2tbsp olive oil
- × 1 red onion, peeled and chopped
- × 1 orange pepper, deseeded and chopped
- × 1 red pepper, deseeded and chopped
- × 6 spring onions, trimmed and chopped

directions

1. To make this chicken thighs recipe, preheat the oven to 200 ° C / 400 ° F / Gas Mark 6. Place the chicken thighs in a roasting pan. Mix the lemon juice, honey and rosemary and brush all over the skin. Grill the chicken for 35-40 minutes until cooked through with a crisp, golden skin.

2. Meanwhile, rinse the quinoa under cool running water. Drain well and place in a pot with 400ml of cold water and bring to a boil. Cover and simmer for 15-20 minutes until all the liquid has been absorbed and the germ has separated from the seed.

3. Heat the olive oil in a frying pan and fry the onion and peppers for 4-5 minutes until they start to soften. Add the quinoa with the chives and season well with salt and freshly ground black pepper. Serve with the roasted chicken thighs.

MELLOW-SPICED CHICKEN AND CHICKPEAS RECIPE

ingredients

- × 8 chicken thighs, skin still on
- × Salt and freshly ground black pepper
- × 1 tbsp olive oil
- × 2 medi onions, peeled and cut into thin wedges
- × 2-4 fat cloves garlic, peeled and crushed
- × 1 tbsp each cumin and coriander seeds and paprika
- × 410g can chickpeas, rinsed and drained
- × 300ml (1/2 pint) hot chicken stock
- × 2-3 tbsp Greek yogurt
- × A handful of fresh coriander leaves, to garnish
- × Bread, to serve

directions

1. Trim excess fat from chicken thighs. Season the meat. Heat the oil in a large skillet, put the thighs skin side down and cook for 8-10 minutes until the skin is a good golden color. Turn them over and cook for another 5 minutes. Remove with tongs and reserve on a plate. Drain all but 1 tablespoon of fat from skillet.

2. Add the onion slices and garlic to the skillet and cook for 5 minutes. Meanwhile, grind the spices in a mortar. Stir them into the skillet and cook for 5 minutes.

3. Add the chickpeas and the broth. Bring to a boil, return the chicken thighs skin side up and simmer, uncovered, for about 15-20 minutes until the chicken is tender.

4. Add tablespoons of Greek yogurt and let it warm, but don't bring it to a boil. Sprinkle with coriander leaves and serve hot with bread.

APPLE CHICKEN STEW

ingredients

- × 1-1/2 teaspoons salt
- × 3/4 teaspoon dried thyme
- × 1/2 teaspoon pepper
- × 1/4 to 1/2 teaspoon caraway seeds
- × 1-1/2 pounds potatoes (about 4 medium), cut into 3/4-inch pieces
- × 4 medium carrots, cut into 1/4-inch slices
- × 1 medium red onion, halved and sliced
- × 1 celery rib, thinly sliced
- × 2 pounds boneless skinless chicken breasts, cut into 1-inch pieces
- × 2 tablespoons olive oil
- × 1 bay leaf
- × 1 large tart apple, peeled and cut into 1-inch cubes
- × 1 tablespoon cider vinegar
- × 1-1/4 cups apple cider or juice
- × Minced fresh parsley

directions

1. Mix the first 4 ingredients. In a 5-quart bottle. slow cooker, vegetable layers; sprinkle with half of the salt mixture.

2. Mix the chicken with the oil and the remaining salt. In a large skillet over medium-high heat, brown chicken in batches. Add to slow cooker. Top with the bay leaf and apple. Add vinegar and cider.

3. Cook, covered, on high for 3 to 3-1 / 2 hours, until chicken is no longer pink and vegetables are tender. Discard the bay leaf. Stir before serving. Sprinkle with parsley.

BUTTER CHICKEN MURG MAKHANI RECIPE

ingredients

- × 450g boneless and skinless
- × For the marinade
- × :
- × 2tsp garlic paste
- × 2tsp ginger paste
- × 1tsp garam masala
- × 150g pot natural yogurt
- × For the sauce:
- × 1tbsp vegetable oil
- × 1 large onion, sliced
- × 2tsp garlic paste
- × 2tsp ginger paste
- × 1tsp garam masala
- × 1/4
- × tsp crushed saffron threads or 1tsp paprika
- × 1 cinnamon stick
- × 500g passata
- × 150ml hot chicken stock
- × 75g butter, melted
- × 50g cashew nut butter
- × Juice 1 lime
- × Handful fresh coriander

directions

1. To make this chicken curry recipe, place the chicken in a plastic food bag with the marinade ingredients and leave it for a good hour (or overnight if possible).

2. To make the sauce, heat the vegetable oil in a large skillet and gently cook the onion for 15 minutes, or until golden brown. Add the garlic ginger pastes and spices and stir 1 min. Pour in the pasta and broth, and simmer for 20 minutes.

3. Heat the grill over medium-high heat. Place the chicken on a wire rack set on a foil lined pan and grill for 10-15 minutes, turning, until cooked through. Let stand, then cut into slices.

4. Remove the cinnamon stick, then puree the sauce. Add the melted butter, cashew butter, and chicken. Season to taste with fresh lime and garnish with fresh coriander.

SOUTHERN-FRIED CHICKEN RECIPE

ingredients

- × 8 mixed organic free-range chicken drumsticks and
- × 75g plain flour
- × 1 organic free-range egg, beaten
- × 35g sachet fajita seasoning
- × 1,ÅÑ2 tsp chilli powder
- × 75g fine polenta
- × 100ml vegetable oil for shallow frying

directions

1. Heat the oven to Mark 6 / 200ÀöC. Place a skillet rack on a large, shallow baking sheet. In a large bowl, mix the chicken with 2 tablespoons of the flour, then dip it into the beaten egg to coat well.

2. In another large bowl, combine the fajita seasoning (reserve 2 teaspoons for the fries), chili powder, polenta, and remaining flour. Add chicken pieces, one at a time, turning to coat well.

3. Heat the oil in a large skillet until hot, add half the chicken and cook for about 3-4 minutes, turning regularly until golden brown. Transfer to a wire rack. Fry the remaining chicken and bake it all together for about 25 minutes, until cooked through.

MANGO CHUTNEY CHICKEN CURRY

ingredients

- × 1 tablespoon canola oil
- × 1 pound boneless skinless chicken breasts, cubed
- × 1 tablespoon curry powder
- × 2 garlic cloves, minced
- × 1/4 teaspoon salt
- × 1/4 teaspoon pepper
- × 1/2 cup mango chutney
- × 1/2 cup half-and-half cream

directions

1. In a large skillet, heat the oil over medium-high heat; brown chicken. Add curry powder, garlic, salt, and pepper; cook until fragrant, 1-2 more minutes.

2. Add the hot sauce and cream. Boil it. Reduce the heat; simmer, uncovered, until chicken is no longer pink, 4 to 6 minutes, stirring occasionally.

CHILLI CHICKEN RECIPE

ingredients

- × 1kg or 8 small boneless
- × , with skin on
- × 100g honey
- × 100g hot chilli sauce (try Mr. Singh's Hot Punjabi Chilli Sauce)
- × 100g balsamic vinegar
- × 2tbsp olive oil
- × Mixed salad leaves, to serve
- × You'll also need:
- × Large mixing bowl
- × Large oven-proof roasting pan

directions

1. Preheat the oven to 200 ° C / 400 ° F / gas 6

2. Add the hot chili sauce to a large bowl.

3. Add the honey and balsamic vinegar and mix well.

4. Add the chicken to the bowl, coating it well with the marinade. Marinate for 15 minutes.

5. Give the base of the pan to roast a light layer of olive oil. Place the chicken on the roasting pan and bake in the oven for 15-20 minutes or grill until perfectly cooked.

6. Serve hot with mixed salad leaves.

SIMPLE FRIED CHICKEN BREAST CUTLETS

ingredients

- × 1 large egg
- × 3/4 cup milk
- × 1 to 2 tablespoons hot sauce, such as Frank's Red Hot, Texas Pete, or Tabasco
- × 1 cup all-purpose flour
- × 1 teaspoon Cajun seasoning, or a similar blend, preferably salt-free
- × 1 teaspoon kosher salt, or 1/2 teaspoon if the Cajun seasoning contains salt
- × 1 teaspoon ground black pepper
- × Vegetable oil, canola, or peanut oil, for frying
- × 2 large boneless, skinless chicken breasts sliced in half lengthwise, or 4 small chicken breasts lightly flattened

directions

1. Gather the ingredients.
2. Ingredients for simple fried chicken cutlets
3. In a large bowl, combine the milk, egg, and hot sauce.
4. Egg, milk and hot sauce mixed in a bowl
5. In a wide, shallow bowl, combine the flour, Cajun seasoning, salt, and pepper.
6. Flour and seasonings combined in a bowl
7. In a large, heavy, deep skillet or Dutch oven, heat about 1 inch of oil to 350 F / 180 C / Gas Mark 4.
8. Oil in a frying pan
9. Preheat the oven to 200 F if you are not serving the chicken cutlets immediately or if you are doubling the recipe and cooking in batches.
10. When the oil is hot, dip a chicken cutlet in the egg-milk mixture, coating both sides. Let the excess drain off and then coat it with the flour mixture. Carefully lower the battered chicken into the hot oil. Repeat with the remaining pieces.
11. Chicken dipped in egg mixture then flour mixture
12. Fry the chicken for about 3 to 4 minutes on each side, until golden brown and cooked through.
13. Fried chicken in a frying pan
14. Drain the chicken on layers of paper towels or brown paper bags. Once the oil returns to temperature, repeat with the remaining chops.
15. Chicken drained on paper towels
16. Serve immediately or transfer to a large baking sheet and keep warm in a 200 F oven or warming drawer. Enjoy.

BAKED CHICKEN WITH BACON AND PEPPER JACK CHEESE

ingredients

- × 4 strips bacon
- × 4 boneless, skinless chicken breasts (halves)
- × 4 tablespoons all-purpose flour
- × 1 tablespoon butter
- × 1 tablespoon olive oil
- × 1/2 clove garlic
- × 4 tablespoons barbecue sauce (thick)
- × 4 slices pepper jack cheese
- × Optional: salt (to taste)
- × Optional: black pepper (to taste)
- × Optional: chili powder (to taste)
- × Garnish: chopped fresh cilantro

directions

1. Gather the ingredients.

2. Grease a baking dish and reserve. Heat oven to 375 F.

3. Fry or bake the bacon until almost crisp. Remove to paper towels to drain. Cook the bacon the day before and refrigerate it for even faster prep time.

4. Pat the chicken dry. Place half a chicken breast between sheets of plastic wrap and mash to a uniform thickness of about 1/4 to 1/2 inch. Repeat with the remaining chicken breast halves. Drain the flour to cover completely.

5. In a large skillet over medium heat, melt the butter with the olive oil. Add half the garlic, stirring into the butter mixture. Remove the garlic and discard it after about 30 seconds.

6. Add the chicken to the skillet and cook for about 5 minutes on each side, until well browned. It should register 165 F on an instant read thermometer.

7. Place the chicken breasts in the baking dish. Spread about 1 tablespoon thick barbecue sauce over each chicken breast half. Top with a slice or two of bacon. Cut the bacon slices in half to coat the chicken. Top the bacon with a slice of pepper jack cheese.

8. Bake the chicken for about 5 to 6 minutes, until the cheese is melted.

9. Sprinkle with cilantro just before serving, if desired.

10. Serve and enjoy!

PAPRIKA CHICKEN WITH SOUR CREAM GRAVY

ingredients

- × 2 tablespoons extra virgin olive oil
- × 4 chicken breasts (on the bone, with skin)
- × kosher salt and freshly ground black pepper
- × 2 teaspoons sweet paprika
- × 1 large onion (or 2 medium onions), sliced
- × 1 cup chicken broth
- × 1/2 cup sour cream mixed with 2 teaspoons flour

directions

1. Heat oven to 400 F. Lightly grease large baking dish and set aside.

2. Heat the olive oil in a large skillet or skillet.

3. Sprinkle the chicken breasts on both sides with kosher salt and freshly ground black pepper.

4. Brown the chicken breasts in the hot oil.

5. Spread sliced onions in bottom of prepared baking dish. Place the chicken on top of the onions and sprinkle the breasts evenly with the paprika.

6. Pour the broth over the chicken.

7. Bake 45 to 55 minutes or until chicken breasts register at least 165 F on an instant read thermometer.

8. Transfer the chicken to a plate and cover loosely with aluminum foil to keep warm.

9. Skim the fat from the juices left in the baking dish, then strain the liquid or put it in a sauce separator.

10. Place the strained juices in a saucepan (or use the baking dish if it is stove-safe). Bring the liquids to a boil over medium-high heat. Lower the heat to low and simmer for 3 to 4 minutes to reduce the liquid and concentrate the flavors.

11. Add the sour cream and flour mixture and heat, whisking constantly, until smooth and thick. Don't let it boil.

12. Serve the sauce with the chicken. If you prefer skinless meat, simply peel off the skin and discard it before coating the breast with sauce.

EASY SKILLET CHICKEN WITH VELOUTE SAUCE

ingredients

- × 1 1/2 pounds boneless, skinless chicken breast (halves)
- × 1/4 cup all-purpose flour
- × 1 teaspoon ground thyme
- × 3/4 teaspoon salt
- × 1/4 teaspoon ground black pepper
- × Dash garlic powder
- × 1 tablespoon olive oil
- × 1 tablespoons butter
- × For the Veloute Sauce:
- × 3 tablespoons butter
- × 2 tablespoons finely chopped shallot or onion
- × 3 tablespoons all-purpose flour
- × 1 1/2 cups chicken stock
- × Dash salt (or to taste)
- × Dash pepper (or to taste)

directions

1. Gather the ingredients.

2. Place chicken breasts between sheets of plastic wrap and mash to a uniform 1/2-inch thickness.

3. In a large skillet, melt 1 tablespoon of the butter with the olive oil.

4. In a shallow bowl or plate, combine the flour, thyme, 3/4 teaspoon salt, 1/4 teaspoon black pepper, and a pinch of garlic powder. Stir to mix well. Drain the chicken pieces into the flour mixture, coating well, then fry for about 4 to 5 minutes on each side, or until chicken is cooked through. The chicken should read at least 165 degrees on an instant read thermometer.

5. Meanwhile, in a saucepan, melt 3 tablespoons of butter. Sauté the onion until tender. Add the 4 tablespoons of flour and stir until well mixed and bubbly. Add the chicken broth and cook, stirring, until thickened. Add salt and pepper to taste.

6. Serve the veloute sauce with the browned chicken pieces.

SIMPLE OVEN-FRIED CHICKEN BREASTS WITH GARLIC

ingredients

- × 2 tablespoons butter
- × 3 tablespoons extra virgin olive oil
- × 1 1/2 pounds chicken breasts (boneless, skinless, 4 halves)
- × Kosher salt (to taste)
- × Freshly ground black pepper (to taste)
- × 1/2 cup all-purpose flour
- × 1 teaspoon garlic powder
- × 1 teaspoon paprika

directions

1. Gather the ingredients.
2. Ingredients for Garlic Baked Chicken Breasts
3. Heat the oven to 400 F / 200 C.
4. Put the butter and olive oil on an 8- or 9-inch square baking sheet (or a skillet large enough to fit the chicken without crowding); place it in the oven to melt the butter. This should only take 1 to 2 minutes, so watch closely to make sure you don't burn.
5. Heat the butter in a baking dish.
6. When the butter in the skillet melts and sizzles, remove the pan from the oven, the butter melted in the pan.
7. Pat the chicken dry with paper towels and remove excess fat.
8. Pat the chicken dry, sprinkle with salt and freshly ground black pepper.
9. Sprinkle with salt
10. Put the flour, garlic powder, and paprika in a cake bowl or plate. Stir to mix well.
11. Put the flour, garlic and paprika in a bowl
12. Dredge the chicken breasts in the flour mixture.
13. Put the chicken breast in the flour mixture.
14. Place them in the hot skillet and return the skillet to the oven. (Don't forget your oven mitts!)
15. Place them in a pan
16. Bake the chicken for 15 minutes.
17. Gently flip the chicken with a spatula and return it to the oven for another 10 to 15 minutes. Chicken should register at least 165 F / 73.9 C on a food thermometer in the thickest pieces.
18. Turn the chicken carefully
19. Serve with the sides of your choice and enjoy!

SKILLET CHICKEN WITH BACON AND SOUR CREAM

ingredients

- × 4 to 6 slices,
- × bacon (drippings reserved)
- × Kosher salt (to taste)
- × Freshly ground black pepper (to taste)
- × 4 to 6 chicken breast halves
- × 2 to 3 tablespoons all-purpose flour
- × 1 tablespoon butter
- × 4 green onions (thinly sliced)
- × 1 clove garlic (minced)
- × 1 cup‚Äã chicken broth
- × 1/2 cup sour cream
- × 1 tablespoon parsley (fresh chopped)

directions

1. Gather the ingredients. Ingredients of the chicken and bacon recipe. Cook the bacon in the oven. Grilled bacon

2. Once done, drain on a paper towel then dice, reserving the bacon fat for later.

3. Bacon and fat. Punch the chicken breasts between sheets of plastic wrap until thin and uniform in thickness. We like them about 1/2 inch thick as they also help the chicken cook more evenly and quickly.

4. Plastic on the chicken breast to mash. Sprinkle the chicken with salt and pepper and lightly sprinkle with flour.

5. Chicken sprinkled with salt and pepper. Put a few teaspoons of the bacon fat and 1 tablespoon of the butter in a large skillet or skillet over medium heat. When the butter is frothy, add the chicken breasts.

6. Chicken stir fry in a skillet. Cook the chicken for about 4 minutes on each side, until golden brown. Chicken cooked in a frying pan. Remove the chicken to a plate and add the green onions and garlic to the skillet.

7. Chicken on a plate. Cook, stirring, for about 1 minute, until onion is soft. Remove the onion mixture to a bowl and set aside.

8. Green onions in a frying pan. Return the chicken to the skillet and add the chicken broth. Bring to a boil. Reduce heat, cover, and simmer for about 5 minutes.

9. Chicken cooked in a pan with broth. Remove the lid, add the diced bacon and onion mixture, and continue to cook for 1 to 2 minutes, until hot. Chicken cooked in broth, green onions and bacon.

10. With a slotted spoon, remove the chicken and bacon mixture to a serving plate. Chicken and bacon on a plate. Stir sour cream into remaining liquid, cook and stir until hot and well mixed. Do not boil.

11. Sour cream mixture in a skillet. Pour sour cream mixture over chicken and bacon. Bacon Sour Cream Skillet Chicken

12. Before serving, garnish the chicken with chopped fresh parsley. Serve hot and enjoy!

RHONDA'S MARINATED CHICKEN SAUCE

ingredients

× 1 c. soy sauce 3 c. water

× 3 tbsp. dark Karo syrup 1/2 tsp. ground ginger

× 5 - 6 cloves garlic, minced 1 tsp. worcestershire sauce

× 4 whole chicken breasts, skinned and boned

directions

1. Marinate chicken at least 4 hours. Grill on low for 1 hour.

CHICKEN BREASTS WITH CREAMY PARMESAN SAUCE

ingredients

- × 4 to 6 chicken breast halves (boneless, without skin)
- × Salt (to taste)
- × Black pepper (to taste)
- × 1 to 2 tablespoons olive oil
- × For the Sauce:
- × 2 tablespoons butter
- × 2 cloves garlic (finely minced)
- × 4 green onions (thinly sliced)
- × 4 ounces cream cheese
- × 1 cup milk (or half-and-half)
- × 1 cup parmesan cheese (freshly shredded; about 2/3 to 3/4 cup grated)
- × 1/8 teaspoon black pepper

directions

1. Gather the ingredients. Chicken with creamy ingredients of Parmesan sauce.

2. Place chicken breasts between plastic wrap sheets or in a plastic food storage bag and gently pat to thin evenly.

3. Mash the chicken in plastic wrap. Lightly sprinkle the chicken breasts with salt and pepper.

4. Heat the olive oil in a large skillet over medium heat.

5. Heat the olive oil in a frying pan.

6. Add the chicken and cook for about 5 to 6 minutes on each side, until well browned and cooked through. The juices should run clear when the thickest part of a chicken breast is cut with a knife.

7. Cook chicken on both sides in a skillet. The minimum safe temperature for chicken is 165 F. Try an instant read thermometer inserted into the thickest portions. Chicken breasts can become dry if overcooked.

8. Chicken breast finished in a skillet. Next, you will make the sauce. For the sauce. Gather the ingredients. Meanwhile, in a saucepan, melt the butter over medium-low heat.

9. Melt the butter in a saucepan. Sauté the garlic and chives for about 1 minute. Sauté the garlic and chives.

10. Add the cream cheese, milk or half and half, and Parmesan cheese and heat until hot and smooth.

11. Add the cream cheese, milk or half and half, and Parmesan cheese and warm

12. Add the pepper and salt to taste. Add salt and pepper to the sauce. Pour sauce over chicken and garnish with parsley. Serve the sauce over the chicken and garnish with parsley. Serve and enjoy!

TARRAGON CHICKEN SALAD

ingredients

- × For the Chicken:
- × 4 chicken breasts (boneless, skinless)
- × 1 tablespoon olive oil
- × Pinch of salt and ground black pepper
- × For the Dressing:
- × 1/2 cup mayonnaise
- × 1/4 cup plain Greek yogurt
- × 2 tablespoons lemon juice (fresh-squeezed)
- × 1 teaspoon Dijon mustard
- × 2 tablespoons fresh tarragon (chopped)
- × 3 stalks celery (small diced)
- × 1/4 red onion (peeled and small diced)
- × For the Salad:
- × 2 cups assorted salad greens
- × Crackers or toasted bread

directions

1. Gather the ingredients. Preheat the oven to 350 F.

2. Rub the chicken breasts with the olive oil and place them on a baking sheet. Sprinkle with salt and pepper. Bake them in the oven for 35-40 minutes, until the chicken is cooked through. Set aside to cool.

3. Once the chicken has cooled, cut it into cubes or shred it with two forks.

4. Make the dressing by mixing together the mayonnaise, Greek yogurt, fresh lemon juice, Dijon mustard, and chopped fresh tarragon. Incorporate the diced celery, diced onion and chicken. Taste and season with more salt and pepper as needed.

5. Serve the chicken salad on a bed of mixed salad along with crackers or toast and fresh seedless grapes.

OVEN-ROASTED CHICKEN WITH PEPPER JELLY GLAZE

ingredients

- × 4 chicken breast halves (bone-in)
- × spicy chicken seasoning blend or a seasoned salt blend and ground black pepper
- × 1 cup red pepper jelly
- × 1 tablespoon butter
- × 2 teaspoons Dijon mustard
- × dash ground black pepper

directions

1. Gather the ingredients.

2. Preheat oven to 425 F.

3. Line a baking sheet with nonstick aluminum foil.

4. Trim excess skin and fat from chicken breasts. Pat dry and sprinkle with seasoning mix or salt and pepper. Place the chicken, rib side down, in the baking dish. Bake for 20 minutes.

5. Meanwhile, combine the jelly, butter, mustard, and pepper in a saucepan and heat until hot and well mixed.

6. Brush the chicken breasts with about half of the gelatin mixture and return to the oven. Bake for another 10 minutes, or until chicken reaches about 165 F. Brush with remaining gelatin mixture a few minutes before done.

7. Serve and enjoy!

AIR FRYER CHICKEN TENDERS

ingredients

- × 1 pound boneless skinless chicken breasts (cut into 1-inch wide strips)
- × 1 cup dill pickle juice
- × 1 large egg
- × 1 cup milk
- × 2 teaspoons salt (divided)
- × 1 1/2 cups flour
- × 1 tablespoon powdered sugar
- × 2 teaspoons ground black pepper
- × 1/2 teaspoon onion powder
- × 1/2 teaspoon paprika

directions

1. Air Fryer Chicken Tenders. Add the tender chicken pieces to a bowl or plastic bag. Pour pickle juice over the top. Cover and refrigerate for at least 30 minutes or up to 3 hours. Do not marinate overnight.

2. Marinate chicken fillets. Whisk together the egg, milk, and 1 teaspoon of the salt in a shallow bowl.

3. Mix of egg and whipped milk. Whisk together the flour, powdered sugar, black pepper, onion powder, paprika, and the remaining teaspoon of salt in a shallow bowl.

4. Dry ingredients shaken together. Rain the chicken strips and dip them into the dry mix. Shake off excess flour.

5. Tender chicken bathed in a flour mixture. Dip them in the egg mixture. Cover each tender completely.

6. Tender chicken in a mixture of egg and milk. Dip them back into the dry mix. Shake off excess flour. Make sure to cover completely with flour. You don't want any humid place. This will cause the shopkeepers to stick to the fryer basket.

7. Tender breaded chicken. Preheat the fryer to 400 F. Grease the fryer basket with olive oil generously to prevent sticking. Add a single layer of the tender ones and drizzle with olive oil spray.

8. Chicken tenders in deep fryer

9. Fry for 15 minutes. Pause in the middle and flip the offers. Spray them again with the olive oil spray and finish cooking.

10. Fryer Cooked Chicken Tenders

11. Repeat with the rest of the chicken fillets. Serve with your favorite sauces.

INSTANT POT CHICKEN BREAST

ingredients

- × 6 (8-ounce) pieces boneless chicken breasts
- × 1 teaspoon kosher salt
- × 1/4 teaspoon black pepper
- × 1 1/2 cups chicken stock
- × 2 cloves garlic (minced)
- × 1 bay leaf
- × Optional: fresh herb sprigs

directions

1. Pat chicken breasts dry with paper towels to dry. Sprinkle the chicken breasts with salt and pepper and place in the Instant Pot.

2. Add the chicken broth, garlic, bay leaf, and herbs, if using.

WINE CHICKEN

ingredients

- × 1 can cream of chicken soup
- × 1 pkg. onion soup mix
- × 1/2 c. red cooking wine

directions

1. Put the ingredients in a heavy skillet.

2. Put the chicken parts on top.

3. Cover and bake for 1 1/2 to 1 3/4 hours at 350 degrees.

CHICKEN POT PIE

ingredients

- × 2 (10 3/4 oz.) cans cream of potato soup
- × 1 (16 oz.) can or pkg.
- × Drained mixed vegetables
- × 2 c.
- × Cooked, diced chicken OR 4 to 5 Market Day chicken steaks, cooked 1/2 c. milk
- × 1/2 tsp. thyme
- × 1/2 tsp. black pepper
- × 2 (9 inch) frozen pie crusts, thawed

directions

1. Combine first 6 ingredients.
2. Spoon into prepared pie crust.
3. Cover with top crust; crimp edges to seal. Slit top crust.
4. Bake at 375 degrees for 40 minutes. Cool 10 minutes. (6 servings)

MOZZARELLA CHICKEN

ingredients

- × 4 whole chicken breasts (boneless)
- × 4 eggs
- × Italian breadcrumbs
- × 3/4 lb. margarine
- × 1/2 lb. fresh mushrooms
- × 1/2 lb. Mozzarella cheese

directions

1. Cut the breasts into serving size pieces.

2. Place the chicken in a lightly beaten egg for 1 hour. Refrigerate. Sauté the mushrooms and reserve.

3. Roll the chicken pieces in breadcrumbs and fry in margarine until golden brown (10 minutes).

4. Place the chicken on a 9 x 13 plate and put the mushrooms on top.

5. Heat the oven to 325 degrees.

6. Bake for 10 to 15 minutes. Then add cheese on top.

7. Put the chicken back in the oven until the cheese is melted.

BAKED CHICKEN PARMESAN

ingredients

- × 2 broiler fryers (2 1/2 lb. each) or equivalent pounds in chicken breasts
- × 2 1/4 c. breadcrumbs
- × 2/3 c. Parmesan cheese
- × 3 tbsp. parsley
- × 1 tsp. salt
- × 3/4 c. butter
- × 1 tsp. Dijon mustard
- × 1/2 tsp. Worcestershire
- × 1 sm. garlic clove

directions

1. Preheat oven to 350 degrees. Rinse chicken and pat dry.

2. Combine crumbs, cheese, parsley and salt. In saucepan, melt butter; beat in mustard, Worcestershire and garlic.

3. Dip chicken in butter, then roll in crumbs. Pat in shallow pan.

4. Bake 1 hour or until golden.

CHICKEN AND ZUCCHINI WITH GARLIC CREAM SAUCE

ingredients

- × 1/4 cup butter
- × 6 chicken breasts
- × salt to taste (kosher)
- × black pepper to taste
- × 3 cups zucchini (sliced 1/8-inch thick)
- × 1/2 cup green onions (diced)
- × For the Garlic Cream Sauce:
- × 2 tablespoons butter
- × 1 large clove garlic (minced; or 2 medium)
- × 3 tablespoons all-purpose flour
- × 3 ounces cream cheese
- × 1 3/4 cups chicken broth
- × 1/2 teaspoon black pepper
- × salt to taste (kosher)

directions

Chicken and Vegetables

1. In a skillet or skillet over medium heat, melt 1/4 cup butter; add chicken breasts; Sprinkle with salt and pepper.

2. Cook for about 3 minutes on each side or until chicken is golden brown.

3. Add the zucchini and sliced onion. Continue cooking, stirring until the zucchini are crisp-tender.

Garlic Cream Sauce

4. In a 2-quart saucepan over medium-low heat, melt 2 tablespoons butter; add the garlic.

5. Cook for 1 minute, then add the flour and cook until soft and bubbly. Continue cooking 1 to 2 more minutes.

6. Add cream cheese, chicken broth, and pepper and continue cooking, stirring occasionally, until sauce is smooth and thick. Taste and add salt as needed.

7. Serve the dish on a bed of rice or pasta. Place the zucchini and then the chicken breasts on top and then pour a little sauce over each chicken breast.

CHICKEN WITH LEMON AND SPICY SPRING ONIONS

ingredients

- × 1 lemon
- × 2 3 1/2 -4-lb. chickens
- × Kosher salt, freshly ground pepper
- × 2large red onions, quartered
- × 2bunches spring onions or 3 bunches scallions, trimmed, divided
- × 4green garlic bulbs, very finely chopped, or 4 garlic cloves, finely grated
- × 1/2 cup extra-virgin olive oil
- × 1/2 cup (1 stick) unsalted butter
- × 6-8 1-thick slices crusty bread
- × 1/4 cup parsley leaves with tender stems
- × Crushed red pepper flakes (for serving)"

directions

1. Preheat the oven to 350C. Cut 1 lemon into very thin slices; pluck seeds. Place chickens on rimmed baking sheet; season inside and out with salt and black pepper. Sprinkle red onions, three-quarters of chives, and half a lemon wedge around.

2. Cook green garlic, oil, and butter in small saucepan over medium heat, stirring occasionally, until butter is melted and garlic begins to sizzle slightly; Season with salt and black pepper. Pour over the chickens, letting a little of the mixture drip over the onions and lemon.

3. Roast chickens, toss in onions and lemon, and drizzle chickens with the fat on a baking sheet occasionally, until chickens are golden all over, an instant read thermometer inserted into the thickest part of the breast registers 160C, and the onions and the lemon soften and begin to harden. brown, 80 minutes-2 hours.

4. Remove the baking sheet from the oven and transfer the chickens to a cutting board, leaving the onions and lemon behind. Place the bread slices on a baking sheet and flip them once to coat with the chicken fat. Return the baking sheet with the bread and vegetables to the oven and broil until the vegetables start to sizzle and crisp and the bread is toasted, 10 to 15 minutes. Meanwhile, thinly slice the remaining chives and toss in a medium bowl with the remaining parsley and lemon wedges. Season with salt, black pepper, and enough red pepper flakes to achieve the desired level of spiciness.

5. Slice chickens and transfer to a large, shallow bowl or bowl (or serve directly on cutting board). Pour the remaining juices on the baking sheet over the chicken and sprinkle on the roasted onions and lemon wedges, followed by the raw chive mixture. Cut each toast into chunks and serve together.

6. Short Ribs with Crispy Garlic and Chili Oil

CHICKEN – BROCCOLI CASSEROLE

ingredients

- × 1 can (10 3/4 oz.) cream of mushroom soup
- × 1 can (10 3/4 oz.) cream of celery soup
- × 1 c. mayonnaise or milk 1 tsp. lemon juice
- × 1 bag (20 oz.) frozen broccoli cuts (thawed & drained)
- × 3 lb. (8 c.) cooked chicken (in sm. pieces)
- × 1 c. shredded Cheddar cheese (4 oz.)
- × 1 can (2.8 oz.) French fried onions

directions

1. Heat the oven to 350 degrees. Lightly grease 2 shallow baking dishes (2 quarts). Whisk the soups undiluted, mayonnaise, and lemon juice in a bowl until well blended.

2. Place half a broccoli in the bottom of each baking dish.

3. Top with half the chicken.

4. Pour soup mix over each; spread to cover; sprinkle with cheese.

5. Bake 25 to 30 minutes until lightly

6. Golden. Sprinkle onions on top.

7. Bake 5-7 more minutes. To freeze: chill, wrap tightly in foil and freeze for up to 3 months. To reheat a baked, frozen wrapped casserole for 1 1/2 hours at 350 degrees. Unwrap and bake 10 more minutes. Chapter KQ, IL Presented by Colleen Wise

BAKED CHICKEN SALAD

ingredients

- × 2 c. cubed chicken
- × 2 c. celery, sliced
- × 1 (10 oz.) pkg. frozen green peas
- × 1/2 c. slivered almonds
- × 2 tbsp. green pepper
- × 1 tbsp. grated onion
- × 2 tbsp. diced pimento
- × 2 tbsp. lemon juice
- × 1/2 tsp. salt
- × 3/4 c. mayonnaise
- × 1 c. grated American cheese

directions

1. Combine all ingredients thoroughly. Turn into buttered 2-quart casserole.

2. Sprinkle with cheese and bake at 350 degrees for 25 minutes or until cheese is melted.

3. Makes 10 servings and this can be frozen.

BARBECUE CHICKEN

ingredients

- × 1 bottle Kraft's Russian dressing
- × 1 pkg. Lipton onion soup mix (dry)
- × 1 jar apricot preserves

directions

1. Pour dressing in bowl.

2. Mix in soup and preserves. Spread over chicken parts.

3. Marinate all day or overnight. Either bake or broil.

CHICKEN TURNOVERS

ingredients

- × 1 pkg. refrigerated crescent rolls (8 ct. tube)
- × 2 c. chopped cooked chicken
- × 3 oz. cream cheese, softened
- × 3 tbsp. chopped green onion
- × 2 tbsp. milk
- × Dash of pepper (optional)
- × 2 tbsp. margarine, melted
- × 2 tbsp. seasoned crumbs

directions

1. Preheat the oven to 350 degrees. In a large bowl, combine the softened cream cheese, milk, pepper, green onion, and minced chicken. Separate the rolls into 4 six-inch squares.

2. Pour 1/4 of the mixture into each square.

3. Bring the corners together and seal.

4. Place on an ungreased baking sheet. Spread with melted margarine and sprinkle with seasoned breadcrumbs.

5. Bake for 20 to 25 minutes. For 4 people.

CAJUN TURKEY BURGERS

ingredients

- × 1 egg, beaten
- × 1 tbsp. worcestershire sauce 1/2 tsp. salt
- × 1/2 tsp. garlic powder 1/2 tsp. onion powder
- × 1/2 tsp. ground red pepper
- × 1/2 c. seasoned fine dry breadcrumbs 1 lb. ground turkey
- × 6 slices bacon

directions

1. In a large bowl, combine the egg, Worcestershire sauce, salt, garlic powder, onion powder, and red bell pepper.

2. Add breadcrumbs and turkey; mix well. Shape turkey mixture into six 3/4 thick patties. Wrap a strip of bacon around the outside of each patty and secure with a wooden toothpick.

3. Place patties on the unheated rack of a roasting pan.

4. Broil 3 to 4 "from heat for 15 to 18 minutes or until no longer pink and bacon is set.

BRANDIED CHICKEN BREAST

ingredients

- × 4 boned & skinned chicken breast
- × 1/3 c. flour
- × 1/2 tsp. salt Ground pepper
- × 1/4 tsp. tarragon leaves
- × 1/4 c. butter
- × 1/3 c. apricot brandy
- × 3/4 c. chicken broth
- × 1/2 c. sour cream

directions

1. Mix flour, salt, pepper, tarragon, dredge the chicken in the flour mixture.

2. Melt the butter, fry the chicken until golden brown.

3. Add the brandy, call.

4. Add broth, simmer covered for 10 minutes or until done.

5. Add sour cream, warm, and serve.

CAROLYN'S CHICKEN & RICE

ingredients

- × 1 c. cream mushroom soup 1 pkg. dry onion soup mix 1 1/4 cans water
- × 1 c. regular rice, uncooked
- × 4 skinless chicken breasts (can use boneless)

directions

1. Bake covered for 2 hours at 350 degrees.

2. Put rice on bottom of casserole dish, then lay chicken on top of rice.

3. Pour soup and rice mixture on top.

4. Cover. Good do ahead.

CHICKEN CASSOULET

ingredients

- × 1 1/2 c. dry navy beans
- × 1 whole med. sized chicken breast,cut into bite-sized pieces Vegetable cooking spray
- × 4 oz. turkey Polish kielbasa, sliced
- × 2 cloves garlic, minced
- × 1 lg. onion, chopped
- × 1 lg. celery stalk, sliced
- × 3 lg. carrots, sliced
- × 1/4 c. parsley, chopped
- × 1/4 c. dry white wine
- × 1 (8 oz.) can tomato sauce
- × 1 tsp. dried thyme
- × 1 tsp. salt
- × 1/4 tsp. pepper
- × 1 tsp. seasoning salt (optional)
- × 4 c. water

directions

1. Rinse and sort the beans.
2. Cover with 6 cups of water and boil 3 minutes.
3. Remove from heat.
4. Cover and let stand 1 hour.
5. Drain and rinse off the spray. Dutch oven with vegetable oil spray; Add the chicken, sausage, garlic, onion, and celery.
6. Sauté until lightly browned.
7. Add beans, carrots, remaining ingredients, and 4 cups of water. Simmer about 1 hour, stirring occasionally. Check the seasonings. Sometimes I add chicken broth.
8. Makes 10 cups.
9. Very low calories. Approximately 3 g of fat and 35 mg of cholesterol. 260 calories.

Anatomy of the Chicken

FRONT VIEW

DRUMSTICK

BREAST

WING →

SIDE VIEW

BACK VIEW

WING   THIGH

WING   DRUMSTICK

THIGH

ANATOMY OF THE CHICKEN

Head

The head is the talkie part of South Africa's famous walkie-talkies and stewing and braising are the best ways to cook it.

Breast

This very lean cut is best cooked quickly to keep them moist, for instance grilling, frying and braaiing. When stewing for braising breasts, don't overcook them as they will become dry and stringy.

Wing

Wings are high in fat and can withstand heat without becoming dry. They therefore are suited to deep- frying, braaiing and roasting. But however you cook them,

Tail

TAILS The tail is often attached to the thigh. It is packed with flavour because it contains a lot of fat and, thanks to the large skin area, becomes very crispy.

ANATOMY OF THE CHICKEN

Neck

This bony cut has very little meat but is an inexpensive way to flavour sauces and stock.

Thighs

Like drumsticks, thighs will be rather tough if not cooked properly. They have loads of fantastic flavour and are best when roasted or braised slowly or added to stews.

Drumstic

This popular cut could also be tough if it hasn't been cooked for long enough. The delicious dark brown meat particularly takes time and drumsticks taste best when they've been roasted, stewed, braised or braaied.

Feet

The other half of walkie-talkies, chicken feet are bony and low on meat. Once cooked, though, they are tender and can be eaten whole. Braai or grill them if you like crisp, crunchy skin.

HOW MANY CALORIES IN CHICKEN?

Chicken tenders

263 calories per 3.5 ounces (100 grams)

Back

137 calories per 3.5 ounces (100 grams)

Dark meat

125 calories per 3.5 ounces (100 grams)

Light meat

114 calories per 3.5 ounces (100 grams)

HOW MANY CALORIES IN CHICKEN?

Breast

A 3.5-ounce (100-gram) serving of chicken breast provides 165 calories, 31 grams of protein and 3.6 grams of fat.

Thigh

A 3.5-ounce (100-gram) serving of chicken thigh provides 209 calories, 26 grams of protein and 10.9 grams of fat.

Wing

Per 3.5 ounces (100 grams), chicken wings provide 203 calories, 30.5 grams of protein and 8.1 grams of fat.

Drumstick

Per 3.5 ounces (100 grams), chicken drumsticks have 172 calories, 28.3 grams of protein and 5.7 grams of fat.

Skin

While a skinless chicken breast is 284 calories with 80% protein and 20% fat, those numbers **dramatically** shift when you include the skin. One boneless, cooked chicken breast with skin (196 grams) contains: Calories: 386, Protein: 58.4 grams, Fat: 15.2 grams

COOKING METHODS

Grilling

This is one of the more common cooking methods, as it tends to require less added fat.

Baking or roasting

These other common methods are sufficient when you don't have access to a grill.

Broiling

This is similar to grilling, but you usually do it in a standard oven or toaster oven.

Braising

Lightly panfry the chicken and then cook it covered, submerged in liquid, for an extended time at a lower temperature.

COOKING METHODS

Fried

The chicken is submerged in hot cooking oil in either a pan or deep fryer. This creates a crisp outer coating but adds quite a bit of fat.

Baking or roasting

These other common methods are sufficient when you don't have access to a grill.

Boiling

You submerge the meat in boiling water and cook it until the internal temperature reaches 165°F (74°C). This is the leanest method, as it doesn't require added fats. Still, some may find the texture lacking.

Quick Recipes

Lemon Garlic Chicken

Place whole roasting chicken in baker with one whole lemon and one head of garlic (unpeeled) in cavity of chicken. Season with salt and pepper. Cover with lid and cook for 1-1/2 hours at 425°. (Try with an orange too.)

Roasted Turkey Breast

Place turkey breast in baker; place 6-8 small red skinned potatoes, halved, around turkey. Add 1/2 cup white wine and 2 cloves pressed garlic. Season with salt and pepper. Cover with lid. Bake at 350°F for 1-1/2 hours. Uncover for last 15-20 minutes. Let stand 5 minutes before slicing.

Honey Mustard Chicken

Place roasting chicken in the baker and pour fat free honey mustard dressing over the top. Cover with lid. Roast for 1-1/2 hours at 425°F.

3 CHEFS' TIPS
A little know-how can make life in the kitchen a lot easier

Done Yet

There are two ways to check if a chicken breast is done.
The first is to insert the tip of a small knife into the thickest part of the meat. If the juices run clear, it is cooked; if it's still pink,
you need to cook longer. Alternatively, make a small incision in the thickest part of the breast. If the meat is completely white and you don't see any pink meat, the brisket is done. The juices will also be clear. This method also works for testing whole chickens and other chicken pieces.

Slicing chicken breast for stir fry

Place the chicken breast, smooth-side down on a cutting board.
Cut it diagonally into 1 cm strips and halve each strip lengthwise into longer, thinner strips before cutting them diagonally across the fibres to keep it tender.

Butterflying chicken breasts for schnitzels

Place the chicken breast smooth side down on a cutting board. Make a shallow incision along one side and continue as if you were trying to cut the breast into two identical halves. Stop just before cutting it all the way through, so the top and bottom half open like a book. With a meat mallet, tap the thickest part gently until it is finer and more uniform. Butterfly breasts can also be stuffed with any filling you like.

TIPS AND TRICKS

Keeping it Clean

× Once the chicken is thawed, do not refreeze it.

× Do not allow raw chicken to come into contact with other foods, cooked or raw.

× Always wash your hands, utensils, and surfaces that have come in contact with raw chicken with hot, soapy water.

× Keep a separate cutting board for raw meat to avoid cross contamination.

× Always make sure the meat is well cooked to kill any harmful bacteria that may have been lurking.

When buying chicken

Always look for chicken that has an even colour with no blemishes or bruises. The meat should look moist and plump and have a neutral smell. Check that the packaging hasn't been damaged in any way. When buying frozen chicken, make sure that the meat is frozen solid and does not have any soft areas where it has begun to defrost – and do remember to check the sell-by-date too.

Storing Chicken

Always refrigerate or freeze chicken as soon as possible after purchasing it. If the package is damaged or soggy and you are going to cook it within two days, remove the chicken, pat dry with kitchen paper, and place on a plate. Cover with cling film or aluminum foil and place plate on bottom rack of refrigerator. That way you won't contaminate other food if it leaks. If you want to freeze the chicken at home, remove it from the package, pat dry, and seal it in an airtight bag.

TIPS AND TRICKS

Stop Breast Drying

How to stop the breast from drying out when MAKING roast chicken.
Roast the chicken breast-side down for two thirds of the cooking time. This way, all the juices will run down into the breast meat and keep it moist. Once you are ready to crisp the skin, carefully turn the chicken breast-side up and roast until golden.

How Tos and Hacks

Chicken salad. Place chicken breast side up on cutting board. Pull the the leg and thigh away from the body and use your fingers to find the hip joint in the crease. Insert the tip of a large knife into the joint and cut through the skin, meat, and joint to separate the thigh and leg from the body.
Repeat on the other side. Use the same method to separate the leg from the thigh and cut the wings from the body. To remove the chicken breast, cut the breast to divide the carcass in two. Cut all the bone and cartilage from the breasts.
You will now have two of each: thighs, drumsticks, wings, and breasts. Add the carcass to soups, stews or casseroles for flavor and remove the bones just before serving.

How to defrost a whole chicken

Thawing a frozen chicken is best done overnight in the fridge. Place it in a large bowl or on a plate to prevent the juices from dripping in the fridge.
Before cooking it, check inside the cavity to see that there is no more ice. If pressed for time, put the bird in a bucket of cold water in the sink, but be sure to keep the water cold to prevent bacteria from growing.

TIPS AND TRICKS

Getting a golden skin

Check that the skin is completely dry, rub the whole bird generously with oil and season well.
Uncover the chicken 20-30 minutes before the end of the cooking time and place it on a shallow baking tray or on an oven rack on a tray to allow the dry heat to come into contact with as much skin as possible. Roast until the skin is crisp and glassy

Chicken and food poisoning

Raw chicken may contain natural bacteria, which could be dangerous if it hasn't been stored properly. Salmonella and campylobacter, which are linked to food poisoning and gastro, are among the most common.

3 DIPS FOR CHICKEN NUGGETS

Garlic and lemon mayo

Stir 2 finely chopped garlic cloves and zest and juice of 1/2 lemon into 1 cup (250 ml) Mayonnaise.

Tomato relish

Finely chop 3 small sherkins and 3 pickeled onions and stir into 3/4 cup (180ml) tomato sauce.

Sweet and sour

Stir together 3/4 cup (180 ml) pineapple juice, 1/4 cup (60 ml) apple cider vinegar, 1/4 cup (60 ml) brown sugar, 2 tbsp (30 ml) tomato cauce and 1 tbps (15 ml) cornflour. Thicker over a low heat.

Quick Recipes

Chicken Pot Pie

Simmer a couple of boneless, skinless chicken breasts, cool and dice. Microwave diced potatoes, carrots, celery, onion, green beans, or peas.
Combine with cornstarch thickened chicken broth (from simmered chicken), and pour into pie crust lined baker (you can use ready-made Pillsbury), then top with the other crust, crimp, brush with milk , sprinkle with herbs, sesame seeds or a little Parmesan and bake at 350 ° for about 40 min.

Cranberry Chicken

Mix one can of whole berry cranberries w/ can of cream of mushroom soup and one packet of onion soup mix. Pour over top of chicken in baker. Cover with lid, place in oven; bake for 1-1/2 hours at 425.

Chicken and Vegetables

Place chicken (skin on or off) in baker. Place chopped onion, celery and carrots around chicken. Sprinkle with 1/2 package of Good Seasons Italian Dressing mix. Place lid on top. Bake at 350° for 1 hour.

The Chicken Cookbook

Chicken Akademy

Table of Contents

CHICKEN CHOPSTICK	9
CHICKEN & ANDOUILLE SMOKED SAUSAGE GUMBO	10
CHICKEN CASSEROLE	11
CHICKEN DIVAN CASSEROLE	12
CHICKEN DIABLE	13
CHICKEN LASAGNE	14
CHICKEN ROYALE	15
CHICKEN ELIZABETH	16
CHICKEN ENCHILADAS	17
BAKED CHICKEN SALAD	18
CHICKEN BREAST EDEN ISLE	19
CHICKEN MACARONI CASSEROLE	20
CHICKEN PIE	21
CHICKEN SALAD CASSEROLE	22
CHICKEN SHISH - KA - BOBS	23
CHICKEN & SHRIMP CASSEROLE	24
CHICKEN POT PIE	25
CRISPY MUSTARD CHICKEN	26
PRESBYTERIAN CHICKEN CASSEROLE	27
ITALIAN ROAST CHICKEN	28
OVEN FRIED CHICKEN BREASTS	29
SKILLET HERB ROASTED CHICKEN	30
SOUR CREAM CHICKEN CASSEROLE	31
SWEET AND SOUR CHICKEN	32
PAELLA	33
HERBED - TURKEY OR CHICKEN - IN - A - BAG	34
SOUTHWEST TURKEY OR CHICKEN BURGERS	35

FRAN'S CHICKEN CASSEROLE 36
CHICKEN CASSEROLE 37
CASSEROLE CHICKEN 38
20-MINUTE CHICKEN PARMESAN 39
CHICKEN POT PIE 40
NO PEEK CHICKEN 41
CHICKEN NOODLE CASSEROLE 42
ORIENTAL CHICKEN 43
PINEAPPLE GLAZED CHICKEN 44
ITALIAN CHICKEN WITH FRESH VEGETABLES 45
CHICKEN BROCCOLI VEGETABLE SAUTE 46
CHICKEN AND ZITI CASSEROLE 47
GARLIC CHICKEN 48
CHICKEN BREASTS IN CREAM SAUCE 49
HONEY GLAZED CHICKEN (LOWFAT) 50
ORIENTAL CHICKEN TENDERS CURRIED PEANUT CHICKEN 51
CHICKEN AND RICE DINNER 52
SWISS CHICKEN 53
CHICKEN AND WILD RICE 54
CHICKEN NOODLE CASSEROLE 55
CHICKEN BREASTS 56
CHICKEN STIR-FRY FEAST 57
CRUNCHY CHICKEN CASSEROLE 58
ORIENTAL CHICKEN WINGS 59
CHICKEN CASSEROLE 60
FRIED CHICKEN BREAST 61
CHICKEN IN THE GARDEN 62
CHICKEN PARISIENNE 63
LEMON CHICKEN SAUCE 64
ORIENTAL CHICKEN TENDERS CURRIED PEANUT CHICKEN 65
CHICKEN WINGS 66
HOT-N-SPICY CHICKEN WINGS 67

SPICY CHICKEN WINGS 68

CRISPY ORIENTAL CHICKEN WINGS (MICROWAVE) 69

TERIYAKI CHICKEN WINGS 70

ANATOMY OF THE CHICKEN 74

HOW MANY CALORIES IN CHICKEN? 77

COOKING METHODS 78

COOKING METHODS 79

QUICK RECIPES 80

3 CHEFS' TIPS 81

TIPS AND TRICKS 85

3 DIPS FOR CHICKEN NUGGETS 86

QUICK RECIPES 87

CHICKEN CHOPSTICK

ingredients

- × 2 (10 1/2 oz.) cans cream of mushroom soup
- × 1 (3 oz.) can chow mein noodles
- × 1 can or bag cashew nuts
- × 2 c. diced chicken
- × 1/2 c. water
- × 1 1/4 c. celery, cut up
- × 1/4 c. chopped onion Dash pepper

directions

1. Combine water and soup; mixture. Reserve 1/2 of the noodles for the top of the casserole.

2. Add other noodles to the soup mix with celery, walnuts, onion, and chicken and stir lightly.

3. Put the reserve noodles on top.

4. Bake for 20 to 25 minutes in 375 degree oven.

CHICKEN & ANDOUILLE SMOKED SAUSAGE GUMBO

ingredients

- × 1 chicken, cut up Garlic powder Cayenne pepper
- × 1 c. chopped onion
- × 1 c. chopped bell pepper
- × 1 c. chopped celery
- × 1 1/4 c. flour
- × 1/2 tsp. salt
- × 1/2 tsp. cayenne pepper Vegetable oil
- × 7 c. chicken stock
- × 1/2 lb. Andoville sausage or Polish kielbasa in 1/4 cubes
- × 1 tsp. minced garlic
- × 2 c. okra (optional) Hot cooked rice"

directions

1. Trim excess fat from chicken pieces. Rub in garlic powder and cayenne pepper. Let stand 30 minutes. In a bowl combine the onion, bell pepper, and celery. Set aside. Combine the flour, 1/2 teaspoon salt, 1/2 teaspoon garlic powder, and 1/2 teaspoon cayenne pepper in a plastic bag.

2. Add the chicken pieces and shake. Reserve 1/2 cup of flour. In a heavy skillet, heat 1-inch oil to very hot. Fry the chicken until golden brown (5-8 minutes side).

3. Drain on paper towels.

4. Pour cooled oil into a glass measuring cup. Scrape the bottom of the pan and return 1/2 cup of the oil to the skillet.

5. Place skillet over heat; add the remaining 1/2 cup flour. Cook; beat constantly until roux is reddish brown (3-4 minutes). Do not burn yourself.

6. Remove from the heat and add the vegetables.

7. Cook until the vegetables are soft. Scrape the bottom of the pan and place the broth in a large pot. Boil it.

8. Add tablespoons of roux mix at a time. Reduce heat to simmer; Add the Andoville sausage and minced garlic. Cook over low heat for 45 minutes.

9. Chicken cooked with bone; cut the meat into 1/2-inch pieces.

10. Add the chicken. For a main course, serve 1/3 cup of rice in a soup bowl with 1 1/4 cups of gumbo.

CHICKEN CASSEROLE

ingredients

- × 2 c.
- × Cooked diced chicken
- × 1 can water chestnuts
- × 1 can mushrooms
- × 1 can cream of mushroom soup
- × 3/4 c. mayonnaise
- × 1 c.
- × Cooked rice
- × 1 c. chopped celery
- × 1/2 c. slivered almonds
- × 1 c. crushed Ritz crackers
Mixed with 1/2 stick melted margarine

directions

1. Mix all ingredients except Ritz crackers.
2. Place in a 9 x 11-inch saucepan.
3. Sprinkle with cookie crumbs.
4. Bake for 45 minutes at 350 degrees. Bubbly and brown. 6-8 servings.

CHICKEN DIVAN CASSEROLE

ingredients

- × 4 chicken breasts, boiled & deboned & broken into lg. pieces
- × 1 lg. bunch broccoli, cooked
- × 1 tbsp. lemon juice
- × 1/4 tsp. curry
- × 1 c. mayonnaise
- × 1 can cream of celery soup
- × 1 pkg. shredded Cheddar cheese

directions

1. Layer the chicken pieces in the bottom of a greased casserole. Then broccoli.

2. Mix the remaining ingredients and pour over the chicken and broccoli.

3. Top with shredded cheddar cheese.

4. Bake at 350 degrees for about 20-30 minutes.

CHICKEN DIABLE

ingredients

× 6 chicken breasts

× 4 tbsp.

× Melted margarine

× 1/2 c. honey

× 1/4 c. mustard

× 1 tsp. salt

× 1 tsp. curry powder

× 4 strips well done bacon, crumbled

directions

1. Bake chicken in 350-degree oven for 30 minutes. Baste with sauce for the last 15 minutes and finally top with crumbled bacon. Serves 6.

CHICKEN LASAGNE

ingredients

- × 8 oz. lasagna noodles
- × 1 can cream of mushroom soup
- × 2/3 c. milk
- × 1/2 tsp. salt
- × 1/2 tsp. poultry seasoning
- × 8 oz. cream cheese, softened
- × 1 c. cream style cottage cheese
- × 1/3 c. chopped onion
- × 1/4 c. minced parsley
- × 3 c. diced cooked chicken
- × 1 1/2 c. soft bread crumbs, buttered
- × 1/3 c. stuffed sliced olives

directions

1. Cook the noodles until tender, drain and rinse.

2. Combine soup, milk, salt, and poultry seasoning in saucepan and heat. Beat the cheeses together; then mix in the olives, onion and parsley.

3. Place half of the noodles in a buttered 9 x 13 x 2-inch baking dish and spread with half the cheese mixture, half the soup mixture, and half the chicken. Repeat the layers.

4. Top with the crumbs.

5. Bake at 375 degrees for 30 minutes. Let stand 10 minutes before serving. Serves 6-8. Freezes well.

CHICKEN ROYALE

ingredients

- × 4 sm. boneless chicken breasts
- × 1/4 c. flour
- × 1/2 tsp. salt, if desired
- × 1/4 tsp. paprika Pepper
- × STUFFING
- × 4 c. soft breadcrumbs
- × 2 tbsp. onion
- × 1/2 tsp. salt
- × 1/8 tsp. thyme Pepper
- × 4 tbsp.
- × Melted butter
- × 1/2 c. water

directions

1. Mix all the ingredients of the filling. Stuff each breast securely with chopsticks, skewers, or string.

2. Put flour, salt, paprika and pepper in a paper or plastic bag. Shake each piece of chicken to coat. Brush the breasts with melted butter.

3. Bake at 325 degrees for 1 to 1 1/2 hours, flipping once.

4. Sprinkle with parsley. Serve with mushroom sauce.

CHICKEN ELIZABETH

ingredients

- × 6 tbsp. butter
- × 8 boneless chicken breast halves
- × 1 pt. sour cream
- × 8 oz. blue cheese
- × 1 tbsp. Lea & Perrins
- × 3 crushed garlic cloves
Chopped parsley White pepper

directions

1. Preheat the oven to 350 degrees. Grease a 9 x 13-inch baking dish.

2. Melt the butter in a large skillet and brown the chicken.

3. Transfer to prepared dish.

4. Combine sour cream, blue cheese, Lea & Perrins, and garlic in a bowl.

5. Add white pepper to taste.

6. Pour over the chicken.

7. Bake 45 minutes. Sprinkle with parsley and serve over rice or noodles.

CHICKEN ENCHILADAS

ingredients

- × 1 chicken (2-3 lb.) cooked & boned
- × 1 med. onion, chopped
- × 1 can cream of mushroom soup
- × 1 can cream of chicken soup
- × 1 c. chicken broth
- × 1 sm. can chopped mild green chilies
- × 1 pkg. corn tortillas (12)
- × 1 lb. long horn cheese, grated
- × 2-3 tbsp. oleo

directions

1. Brown the chopped onion in oil.

2. Add the soups, chicken broth, and green chilies. Beat until smooth.

3. Add the minced chicken to the sauce. Heat until boiling. Fill each tortilla with salsa and place in a large casserole.

4. Top with grated cheese.

5. Bake at 350 degrees for 20-30 minutes or until bubbly. It can be prepared the night before and cooked before serving the next day. Makes 10-12 servings.

BAKED CHICKEN SALAD

ingredients

- × 1 can cream of chicken soup
- × 2 c.
- × Cooked chicken
- × 3/4 c. mayonnaise
- × 1 tsp. lemon juice
- × 1 c. chopped celery
- × 1/2 sm. onion, diced
- × 1/4 c. chopped pimento
- × 1/2 tsp. pecan or almond, chopped
- × 3 hard boiled eggs, chopped
- × 2 c. crushed potato chips

directions

1. Mix together all ingredients except potato chips.
2. Top with crushed chips.
3. Bake at 400 degrees for 20 minutes until bubbly.

CHICKEN BREAST EDEN ISLE

ingredients

- × 12-14 half chicken breasts, boned
- × 2 jars dried chipped beef
- × 1 (8 oz.) carton sour cream
- × 1 can cream mushroom soup
- × 12-14 slices bacon

directions

1. Wrap slices of bacon around each half of the breast. Hold with a toothpick. Layer the shredded meat in the bottom of the open skillet.

2. Cover with breasts.

3. Top with the soup mixture and sour cream.

4. Bake at 300 degrees, covered with foil for the first hour.

5. Turn to 250 degrees and bake 2 more hours. Baste half the time.

6. Remove the foil to cook for the last 1/2 hour.

7. Remove the toothpicks. A little vermouth or sherry can be added to the above, if desired. (For larger portions, roll 1/2 chicken thigh (boneless) inside the breast portion

CHICKEN MACARONI CASSEROLE

ingredients

- × 1 pkg. uncooked creamette macaroni (7 oz.)
- × 1 can cream of mushroom soup
- × 1 can cream of celery soup
- × 1/2 lb. grated Velveeta cheese
- × 15 oz. can water chestnuts
- × 2 c. diced cooked chicken
- × 1/4 c. diced green pepper
- × 1 (2 oz.) jar diced pimentos
- × 1 sm. can mushroom pieces
- × 1 1/2 c. milk
- × 1 tsp. salt

directions

1. Mix all the ingredients in a large bowl. Refrigerate overnight. Turn it into a 9 x 13-inch glass casserole with butter.

2. Bake at 350 degrees for 1 1/4 hours. Tuna, shrimp, or crab meat can be substituted for chicken.

CHICKEN PIE

ingredients

× 1 chicken, boiled & boned 1 can cream chicken soup 1 1/2 c. chicken broth

× 1 c. flour

× 1 tsp. baking powder 1/2 tsp. salt

× 1 tsp. pepper

× 1 c. milk

× 1stick oleo, melted

directions

1. Combine chicken, soup, and broth.

2. Place on a 9 x 13-inch plate. Make the dough by combining the remaining ingredients.

3. Pour over the chicken mixture.

4. Bake at 425 degrees for 30 minutes.

CHICKEN SALAD CASSEROLE

ingredients

- × 2 c. chopped cooked chicken
- × 1 c. chopped celery
- × 1 can cream of chicken soup
- × 3/4 c. mayonnaise
- × 1 c. sliced diced water chestnuts
- × 1/2 c. slivered almonds
- × 4 tbsp. butter
- × 1 c. crushed corn flakes

directions

1. Mix all ingredients except butter and corn flakes.

2. Place in ungreased 13 x 9 x 2-inch saucepan.

3. Melt the butter and mix with the corn flakes. Spread over the casserole and bake at 350 degrees for 45 minutes.

4. All ingredients can be pre-mixed except corn flakes and butter.

5. This should be placed just before baking.

6. The casserole should be eaten as soon as it is baked.

CHICKEN SHISH - KA - BOBS

ingredients

- × 3 lb. chicken, cut in chunks or strips marinade in mixture of 1/3 c. teriyaki sauce
- × 2 tbsp. vegetable oil
- × 2 tbsp. chili sauce
- × 1/4 c. honey
- × 1 tsp. salt
- × 1/2 tsp. ground ginger
- × 1/4 tsp. garlic powder

directions

1. Alternate skewered chicken with cherry tomatoes, mushrooms, pineapples, chopped green peppers, and chopped onions.

2. Grill and enjoy.

CHICKEN & SHRIMP CASSEROLE

ingredients

- × 1/2 c. flour
- × 1 lg. frying chicken, cut into serving pieces
- × 1 onion, diced
- × 1 clove garlic
- × 1 can tomato sauce
- × 1 tsp. salt
- × 1/2 tsp. pepper
- × 1 tsp. basil
- × 2 tsp. parsley
- × 1 tsp. paprika
- × 1 can minced clams
- × 1/2 lb. mushrooms, sliced
- × 1/4 c. sherry
- × 1/2 lb. shrimp, peeled & deveined

directions

1. Dredge the chicken in flour.

2. Lightly brown in a skillet.

3. Place in a saucepan.

4. Lightly fry the onion.

5. Add the garlic, tomato sauce, salt, pepper, basil, parsley, paprika, clams with the liquid, mushrooms and sherry. Cook over low heat for 10 minutes. Pour the sauce over the chicken. Cover and bake at 350 degrees for 1 hour.

6. When ready to serve, uncover the casserole and add the shrimp.

7. Cover the shrimp with sauce and bake 10 more minutes at 350 degrees. Makes 6 servings. It can be served over rice.

CHICKEN POT PIE

ingredients

- ×   3 cans white meat chicken, drained
- ×   1 can Veg-All, drained
- ×   1 can cream of potato soup
- ×   1 can cream of mushroom soup
- ×   1/2 c. milk or
- ×   1/2 c.
- ×   Cooking sherry Salt & pepper
- ×   2 Pillsbury pie crusts
- ×   1 egg, for egg wash

directions

1. Place 1 crust in bottom of 9-inch pie pan.

2. Use beaten egg in the crust.

3. Mix chicken, Veg-All, soup, milk or sherry, salt and pepper.

4. Place on the crust.

5. Cover with another crust; seal. Use beaten egg and then make cuts.

6. Bake at 350 degrees for 40 minutes.

7. Don't put it on a cookie sheet.

CRISPY MUSTARD CHICKEN

ingredients

- × 2 tbsp. reduced calorie mayonnaise
- × 2 tbsp. prepared mustard
- × 1/4 c. wheat germ
- × 1/3 c. fine dry bread crumbs
- × 1/2 tsp. ground thyme
- × 1/4 tsp. salt
- × 4 (4 oz.) skinned boned chicken breast halves Vegetable cooking spray

directions

1. Combine mayonnaise and mustard in small bowl; stir well.

2. Combine the wheat germ and the next 3 ingredients in a shallow bowl. Spread each chicken breast with the mustard mixture, put it in the breadcrumb mixture.

3. Place chicken in a 10 x 6 x 2-inch baking dish that has been coated with cooking spray.

4. Cover and bake at 350 degrees for 40 minutes.

5. Uncover and bake for an additional 20 minutes or until chicken is tender. 4 portions.

PRESBYTERIAN CHICKEN CASSEROLE

ingredients

× 2 c. chicken, cooked & diced

× 1 can water chestnuts, drained, sliced 1 can LeSueur peas

× 1 can cream of chicken soup 1 c. (lite) sour cream

× 1 tube Ritz crackers, crushed 1 stick oleo, melted

× 2 tbsp. poppy seeds

directions

1. Combine chicken, water chestnuts, peas, soup, and sour cream.

2. Place in greased 7 x 11-inch casserole.

3. Top with crackers mixed with oil and poppy seeds.

4. Bake for 30 minutes at 350 degrees or until bubbly.

ITALIAN ROAST CHICKEN

ingredients

- × 1 fryer, cut up & washed
- × 2-3 tbsp. oil (for baking sheet pan)
- × 2-3 cloves garlic
- × Sage leaves, crumpled Parsley
- × Garlic salt Oregano Salt Pepper

directions

1. Place the chicken on a cookie sheet covered with 2-3 tablespoons of oil. Chop the garlic over the chicken pieces.

2. Sprinkle other seasonings over the chicken.

3. Bake at 350 degrees for about 1 hour.

OVEN FRIED CHICKEN BREASTS

ingredients

× 8 skinless, boneless chicken breast halves

× 1/2 c. plain nonfat yogurt

× 1/2 box Ritz crackers, crushed into fine crumbs

directions

1. Dip chicken in yogurt and roll in cookie crumbs.

2. Place the chicken in a baking dish and bake in the oven at 350 degrees for 30 minutes on each side.

3. Makes 8 servings.

SKILLET HERB ROASTED CHICKEN

ingredients

- × 4 skinless, boneless chicken breast halves
- × 2 tbsp. all-purpose flour
- × 1/4 tsp. ground sage
- × 1/4 tsp. dried thyme
- × 2 tbsp. margarine
- × 1 (10 3/4 oz.) can cream of chicken soup
- × 1/2 c. water

directions

1. On wax paper, combine the flour, sage, and thyme. Coat the chicken lightly with the flour mixture. In a skillet over medium high heat, in hot margarine, cook chicken for 10 minutes or until brown on both sides; push chicken aside.

2. Add the soup and 1/2 cup water, stirring to loosen the browned bits. Reduce heat to low.

3. Cover; simmer 5 minutes or until chicken is tender with fork. Serve over hot cooked rice. For 4 people.

SOUR CREAM CHICKEN CASSEROLE

ingredients

- × 3 c.
- × Cooked, diced chicken
- × 1 (8 oz.) bag noodles
- × 1 sm. can mushrooms
- × 2 cans cream of chicken soup
- × 1 (16 oz.) sour cream
- × 8 oz. Swiss cheese

directions

1. Cook and drain the noodles.

2. Combine all ingredients except Swiss cheese.

3. Place in 9 x 13-inch pan; top with Swiss cheese.

4. Bake at 350 degrees for 45 minutes.

SWEET AND SOUR CHICKEN

ingredients

- × 4 whole chicken breasts, split
- × 4 chicken leg thighs (not split)
- × 1 (18 oz.) jar apricot preserves
- × 1 (8 oz.) bottle Russian dressing
- × 1 env. onion soup mix

directions

1. Place the chicken in a large, shallow baking dish.

2. Combine remaining ingredients and pour over chicken, trying to coat all pieces.

3. Bake at 350 degrees for 75 minutes. Serve with brown rice and pour a little sauce on top. Despite the unusual ingredients, it is delicious.

PAELLA

ingredients

- × 1/2 lb. shrimp, cleaned (chicken can also be used)
- × 2 garlic cloves, crushed
- × 2 tbsp. butter or margarine
- × 1 tbsp. cornstarch
- × 1 1/4 c. chicken broth
- × 1 can (14 1/2 oz.) chopped tomatoes with liquid
- × 1/2 c. sliced pepperoni
- × 1 pkg. (10 oz.) frozen peas, thawed
- × 1/4 tsp. cayenne pepper
- × 1 1/2 c. dry minute rice
- × 1/8 tsp. saffron

directions

1. Sauté shrimp and garlic in butter until shrimp are pink approx. 2 minutes.

2. Add cornstarch and cook 1 minute.

3. Add the broth, tomatoes, pepperoni, peas, and cayenne pepper.

4. Bring to a boil, stirring occasionally.

5. Add the rice and saffron.

6. Cover and remove from heat. Let stand 5 minutes. Stir with a fork.

7. Makes 4 servings.

HERBED – TURKEY or CHICKEN – IN – A – BAG

ingredients

- × 1 (7-10 lb.) turkey or chicken
- × 2 tbsp. dried parsley
- × 1 tbsp. rubbed sage
- × 1 tsp. marjoram
- × 1 tsp. thyme
- × 1 tsp. savory
- × 1/2 tsp. rosemary
- × 1 tbsp. flour

directions

1. Rinse the turkey and pat dry.

2. Combine parsley and next 5 ingredients in blender; process 1 minute.

3. Sprinkle the cavity and exterior of the turkey with the herb mixture. Shake flour in large cooking bag; Place in a large roasting pan at least 2 inches deep.

4. Place the turkey in the bag according to the instructions. Insert the meat thermometer.

5. Bake at 325 degrees until the thermometer reaches 185 degrees.

6. Remove from the oven and cut the bag open.

7. Remove the turkey and let it rest 15 minutes before carving. Serve with dressing. Makes 10-12 servings.

SOUTHWEST TURKEY or CHICKEN BURGERS

ingredients

- × 1 lb. ground turkey or chicken Bottled mild salsa
- × 1/2-3/4 lb. mushrooms
- × 1 tbsp. salad oil
- × 1/2 tsp. salt
- × 2 tbsp. mayonnaise
- × 4 Kaiser rolls or hamburger buns

directions

1. In a bowl, combine ground chicken or turkey and 1/4 cup sauce; form 4 patties. Grill or broil until they lose their pink color turning once.

2. Meanwhile, slice the mushrooms. In a skillet over medium heat, in hot salad oil, cook the mushrooms and salt until lightly browned, stirring frequently. In a small bowl, mix the mayonnaise and 1/3 cup of the sauce.

3. To serve, cut each roll in half. Spread mayonnaise mixture on bottom halves of buns.

4. Top with patties and mushrooms.

FRAN'S CHICKEN CASSEROLE

ingredients

- × 8 chicken breasts, cooked, cubed
- × 1 pkg. wide noodles
- × 1/4 c. butter, melted
- × 1 can cream of mushroom soup
- × 1 can cream of chicken soup
- × 1 pt. sour cream
- × 1 tbsp. sherry
- × 1/4 c. grated onion
- × 1 tsp. seasoned salt Paprika, optional

directions

1. Bake the chicken for 45 minutes in broth and water.

2. Remove chicken, cool, and cover.

3. Cook the noodles in broth and water according to package directions, being careful not to overcook.

4. Drain, put in the bottom of a greased 13 x 9 x 2-inch casserole. Drizzle the butter over the noodles.

5. Mix in all the remaining ingredients except the chicken.

6. Add chicken on top of noodles; then spread the sour cream mixture over everything.

7. Sprinkle the top with paprika. Bake at 350 degrees for 20-30 minutes or until the top is lightly browned and the casserole is piping hot.

CHICKEN CASSEROLE

ingredients

×   2 chicken breasts, cooked and shredded

×   1 bag Pepperidge Farm herb dressing

×   2 cans chicken noodle soup

×   1 can cream of chicken soup

×   3 eggs, beaten

×   1/2 stick butter or margarine, melted

directions

1. Butter a 9 x 13-inch cake pan.

2. Mix 3/4 bag of dressing, chicken, soups, and eggs.

3. Put on a plate. Drizzle with butter and sprinkle with the remaining dressing.

4. Bake at 325 degrees for about 40 minutes.

CASSEROLE CHICKEN

ingredients

- × 1 whole chicken, cut up
- × 1 (8 oz.) sour cream
- × 1 (10 3/4 oz.) can cream of mushroom soup
- × 1 pkg. dry onion soup mix
- × 1 (3 oz.) can chow mein noodles

directions

1. Chop chicken to serve; Place in a saucepan large enough to hold the chicken comfortably.

2. Combine sour cream, mushroom soup, and onion soup mix. Spread soup mix over chicken.

3. Top with chow mein noodles and bake at 325 degrees for 1 1/2 hours.

20-MINUTE CHICKEN PARMESAN

ingredients

- × 4 boneless and skinless chicken breast halves (about 1 lb.)
- × 1 egg, slightly beaten
- × 1/2 c. seasoned breadcrumbs
- × 2 tbsp. margarine or butter
- × 1 3/4 c. Prego spaghetti sauce
- × 1/2 c. shredded Mozzarella cheese
- × 1 tbsp. grated Parmesan cheese
- × 1/4 c. chopped fresh parsley

directions

1. With the palm of your hand, flatten the chicken until it is uniform thickness.

2. Dip the chicken in the egg and then in crumbs to coat. In a skillet over medium heat, in hot margarine, brown the chicken on both sides.

3. Add the Prego sauce. Reduce the fire.

4. Cover; simmer 10 minutes.

5. Sprinkle with cheeses and parsley.

6. Cover; simmer 5 minutes or until cheese is melted. 4 portions.

CHICKEN POT PIE

ingredients

- × 2 (10 3/4 oz.) cans cream of broccoli soup
- × 1 c. milk
- × 1/4 tsp. thyme leaves, crushed
- × 1/4 tsp. pepper
- × 4 c.
- × Cooked cut up vegetables (broccoli, carrots, potatoes, etc.)
- × 2 c. cubed cooked chicken or turkey
- × 1 (10 oz.) can Hungry Jack flaky biscuits 1.

directions

1. In a 3-quart baking dish, combine the soup, milk, thyme, and pepper.

2. Add the vegetables and chicken.

3. Bake at 400 degrees for 15 minutes or until mixture begins to bubble.

4. Meanwhile, cut each cookie into quarters.

5. Remove the dish from the oven; stir. Spoon cookie pieces over hot chicken mixture.

6. Bake for 15 minutes or until cookies are golden brown.

NO PEEK CHICKEN

ingredients

- × 1 pkg. Uncle Ben's wild rice
- × 1 can cream of mushroom soup
- × 1 can cream of celery soup
- × 1 soup can of water
- × 1 tsp. parsley
- × Dash of curry powder
- × 4-6 chicken breasts, boned and skinned
- × 1/2 pkg. Lipton onion soup

directions

1. Preheat the oven to 350 degrees. Grease a 9 x 13-inch baking dish.

2. Mix the first 6 ingredients; Pour into a baking dish. Place the chicken breast on top.

3. Sprinkle soup mix over chicken.

4. Cover tightly with aluminum foil.

5. Bake 2 1/2 hours. Don't watch until they are 2 1/2 hours. Let stand 15 to 30 minutes before serving.

CHICKEN NOODLE CASSEROLE

ingredients

- × 1 can cream of chicken soup
- × 1/2 c. milk
- × 1 pkg. Meullers dumpling noodles (serve 6)
- × 1 (6 oz. or so) can chicken

directions

1. Cook noodles according to package directions.

2. Add the chicken, soup, and milk. Simmer for 15 minutes and serve hot.

3. Additions and substitutions: tuna instead of chicken; cream of mushrooms instead of cream of chicken; peas, corn or your favorite vegetable.

ORIENTAL CHICKEN

ingredients

- × 1/2 c. butter
- × 1/2 c. flour
- × 1 tbsp. salt
- × 1 c. cream
- × 3 c. milk
- × 2 c. chicken stock
- × 2 c. cubed chicken
- × 1/2 c.
- × Sauteed sliced mushrooms
- × 1/2 c. blanched almonds
- × 1 c. sliced water chestnuts
- × 1/4 c. pimento strips
- × 1/4 c. sherry

directions

1. Melt the butter on top of the bain-marie, add the flour and salt, cook until bubbly; Add the cream, milk, and chicken broth, stirring until smooth.

2. Cook over hot water for 30 minutes. Just before serving, add the remaining ingredients and heat well. Serve over soufflé, rice or cheese rind.

PINEAPPLE GLAZED CHICKEN

ingredients

- × 4 chicken breasts, skinned and deboned
- × 1 (15 oz.) can chunk pineapple Scallions to top the meat
- × Salt and pepper
- × 2 tbsp. margarine
- × 1/4 c. packed brown sugar

directions

1. Salt and pepper chicken breasts, brown in margarine over medium heat.

2. When brown add pineapple and sugar.

ITALIAN CHICKEN WITH FRESH VEGETABLES

ingredients

- × 2 skinless, boneless chicken breast, split 1 (16 oz.) can tomatoes
- × 1 sm. can black olives 1 zucchini, sliced
- × 1 summer squash, sliced 1 green pepper, sliced
- × Handful of fresh green beans 1 med. onion, cut in wedges 1/2 tsp. oregano
- × 1/4 tsp. basil Salt and pepper Garlic powder
- × Mozzarella cheese, shredded

directions

1. Season the chicken with salt, pepper, and garlic powder.

2. Brown chicken in large skillet.

3. Cover with tomatoes.

4. Cover the pan and simmer for 20 minutes.

5. Add fresh greens and top with oregano and basil; cover the skillet and continue to simmer for 20 minutes.

6. Add the black olives and top with mozzarella cheese. Continue simmering until cheese is melted. Serve over white rice.

CHICKEN BROCCOLI VEGETABLE SAUTE

ingredients

- × 2 tbsp. margarine, divided
- × 4 skinless, boneless chicken breast halves (about 1 lb.)
- × 1 c.
- × Cut-up broccoli
- × 1/2 c. thinly sliced carrots
- × 1 c. sliced mushrooms
- × 1 can Campbell's cream of broccoli soup
- × 1/3 c. milk
- × 1/8 tsp. pepper

directions

1. In a skillet over medium heat, in 1 tablespoon of hot margarine, cook chicken for 10 minutes or until brown on both sides.

2. Remove the chicken; keeping warm. In the same skillet, with the remaining margarine, cook the broccoli, carrots, and mushrooms for 5 minutes, stirring frequently.

3. Add the soup, milk, and pepper.

4. Heat until boiling. Return the chicken to the skillet. Reduce heat to low; simmer 5 minutes or until chicken is tender with fork. 4 portions. Preparation time: 10 minutes.

5. Cooking time: 20 minutes.

CHICKEN AND ZITI CASSEROLE

ingredients

- × 1 jar spaghetti sauce (any variety)
- × 4 c.
- × Cooked ziti (6 oz. uncooked)
- × 1 1/2 c. cubed cooked chicken or turkey
- × 1 c. shredded Mozzarella cheese
- × 1 tbsp. grated Parmesan cheese

directions

1. Use a 2-quart casserole: mix spaghetti sauce, cooked ziti, chicken, and 1/2 cup mozzarella.

2. Sprinkle with the rest of the mozzarella cheese and Parmesan.

3. Bake at 350 degrees for 30 minutes or until hot and bubbly.

4. Makes 6 servings.

GARLIC CHICKEN

ingredients

- × 1 bottle olive oil
- × 2-3 cloves of garlic
- × Whole chicken, cut up or 5 breasts
- × 6 potatoes, peeled and sliced thin Salt and pepper

directions

1. Preheat the oven to 450 degrees.

2. Pour the olive oil into a 13 x 9-inch pan.

3. Add the garlic cloves.

4. Bake the cloves until they pop.

5. Add the sliced potatoes and chicken pieces. Lower the oven to

6. 400 degrees and bake 45 minutes. Flip the chicken after 30 minutes. Season to taste with salt and pepper.

CHICKEN BREASTS IN CREAM SAUCE

ingredients

- × 4 chicken breasts halves, boned and skinned and rinsed
- × 1/4 c. flour
- × 1/2 tsp. salt
- × 1/2 tsp. pepper
- × 2 tbsp. butter
- × 2 tbsp. vegetable oil
- × 1/4 lb. mushrooms, sliced
- × 3/4 tbsp. garlic, chopped
- × 1 green onion, chopped

directions

1. Add salt, pepper, and flour.

2. Dredge chicken breasts in seasoned flour mixture, shake off excess.

3. Add the butter and vegetable oil to the skillet, cook over medium heat.

4. Cook the chicken breasts for 2 1/2 minutes on each side.

5. Add mushrooms, garlic - cook for about 1 minute more until chicken is almost done, add chopped onion.

6. Drain the fat from the pan and reserve. About 4 servings.

HONEY GLAZED CHICKEN (LOWFAT)

ingredients

- × 1 tbsp. ginger
- × 1/4 c. low-sodium soy sauce
- × 1/2 c. sherry
- × 3 tbsp. finely chopped onion
- × 1 1/2 tbsp. honey
- × 5-6 boneless, skinless chicken breasts

directions

1. Mix together ginger, soy sauce, sherry, onion and honey.

2. Pour on one side of chicken and broil 5 minutes. Turn and pour remaining ingredients on other side of chicken.

3. Broil for 3-5 minutes longer.

ORIENTAL CHICKEN TENDERS CURRIED PEANUT CHICKEN

ingredients

- × 1 c. soy sauce
- × 1/3 c. sugar
- × 4 tsp. vegetable oil
- × 1 1/2 tsp. ground ginger
- × 1 tsp. five spice powder
- × 2 bunches green onion
- × 16 chicken tenders (approx. 2 lbs.)

directions

1. Combine soy sauce, sugar, oil, ginger, and five powdered spices in a large bowl until the sugar dissolves.

2. Add the green onions.

3. Add the chicken fillets to the marinade. Flip to cover.

4. Cover the chicken and refrigerate overnight.

5. Preheat the oven to 350 degrees.

6. Drain the chicken RESERVING THE MARINATE. Place the chicken on a plate and bake until golden and tender, while occasionally drizzling with the marinade.

CHICKEN AND RICE DINNER

ingredients

- × 1 chicken, lg. enough for your whole family Some butter or margarine
- × Salt and pepper
- × Rice

directions

1. Wash the chicken.

2. Pat the skin several times with butter or margarine.

3. Sprinkle with salt and pepper.

4. Bake in 350 degree oven for about 1 hour. Drizzle the chicken after 30 minutes. Rice - Follow the directions for bagged boil rice - it's quick, easy, and delicious.

5. Sauce: When the chicken is done, remove it from the pan.

6. Heat drips on

7. medium heat on the stove. Mix well 1/4 cup of flour with 1/2 cup of water. Gradually add this to the chicken fat while it boils. You may not need all of the flour and water mixture, mix to taste. Boil slowly for 10 minutes over low heat. Serve hot.

SWISS CHICKEN

ingredients

- × 1 stick margarine or butter
- × 1/2 c. milk
- × 10 chicken breast halves,
- × deboned 10 slices Swiss cheese
- × 1 can cream of chicken soup
- × 1 pkg. Pepperidge Farm herb dressing mix (sm.)

directions

1. Place the chicken breast in a large, flat baking dish.

2. Sprinkle with salt and pepper (salt in moderation).

3. Place 1 slice of cheese on top of each breast.

4. Mix can of soup with 1/2 cup of milk and pour over chicken.

5. Melt the margarine or butter and mix with the dressing mix and spread over the chicken.

6. Bake at 325 degrees uncovered for 1 1/2 hours.

CHICKEN AND WILD RICE

ingredients

× 1 (6 oz.) pkg. Uncle Ben's wild rice (original)

× 1 can cream of chicken soup

× 1 can cream of celery soup

× 1 can mushrooms

× 1 whole chicken, cut up

× 1 pkg. Lipton's onion soup mix

directions

1. Butter a 13 x 9 inch pan.

2. Mix together rice, soup and mushrooms and spread in bottom of pan.

3. Place chicken pieces on top of rice mixture and sprinkle with onion soup mix.

4. Cover with foil and bake at 350 degrees for about 1 1/2 hours. Serves 4-5.

CHICKEN NOODLE CASSEROLE

ingredients

- × 1 sm. pkg. egg noodles
- × 1 can cooked chicken, drained
- × 1 can cream of chicken soup
- × 1 soup can milk
- × Butter
- × Bread crumbs Salt and pepper

directions

1. Cook noodles in boiling water.

2. Drain.

3. Combine soup, milk, chicken, salt and pepper in saucepan.

4. Bring just to a boil. Take off heat and add to noodles in buttered casserole dish.

5. Sprinkle with bread crumbs.

6. Bake in 300 degree oven for approximately 30 minutes or until bubbly and brown.

CHICKEN BREASTS

ingredients

× 4 chicken breasts, halved and boned

× 8 slices Swiss cheese

× 1/3 pkg. Pepperidge Farm stuffing

× 1 can cream of chicken soup

× 1/4 c. milk

× 1/4 c. margarine

directions

1. Place chicken breasts, skin side down, in 9 x 13-inch skillet. Place a slice of cheese on each piece. Dilute the soup with milk and divide the mixture evenly in each piece.

2. Melt the margarine.

3. Mix with the dressing and sprinkle on top.

4. Cover.

5. Bake at 325 degrees for 2 hours. Uncover the last 40 minutes.

CHICKEN STIR-FRY FEAST

ingredients

- × 1 c. raw Uncle Ben's original converted brand rice
- × 1 lb. boneless, skinless chicken breasts
- × 3 tbsp. cornstarch, divided
- × 3 tbsp. soy sauce, divided
- × 3 tbsp. dry sherry, divided
- × 1 lg. clove garlic, minced
- × 4 tbsp. peanut oil or safflower oil, divided
- × 1 lg. carrot, julienned
- × 1 lg. green or red bell pepper, cut into strips
- × 1 lg. onion, sliced
- × 1/4 lb. fresh mushrooms, sliced

directions

1. Cook rice according to package directions. Meanwhile, cut chicken into 1-inch square pieces; Combine with the mixture of 2 tablespoons cornstarch and 1 tablespoon soy sauce, sherry, and garlic. Let stand 30 minutes.

2. Mix remaining cornstarch, sherry, and 2/3 cup water; set aside.

3. Heat 2 tablespoons of oil in a hot wok or large skillet until hot.

4. Add the chicken and sauté for 4 minutes; remove.

5. Heat the remaining oil in the same skillet.

6. Add the carrots, bell pepper and onion; sauté 4 minutes.

7. Add the mushrooms; sauté for 30 seconds.

8. Add the chicken and cornstarch mixture.

9. Cook, stirring, until sauce comes to a boil and thickens.

10. Remove from heat; add the rest of the soy sauce. Serve over rice.

CRUNCHY CHICKEN CASSEROLE

ingredients

- × 2 cans boned chicken, drained
- × 1 can cream of chicken soup
- × 1 soup can evaporated milk
- × 1 sm. can mushrooms, drained
- × 1 1/4 c. minute rice
- × 1/2 stick margarine, sliced
- × 1/2 c. slivered almonds

directions

1. Mix and place in casserole dish.
2. Bake 45 minutes at 375 degrees.

ORIENTAL CHICKEN WINGS

ingredients

× 6 chicken wings 1 sm. clove garlic 1 scallion

× 1/4 c. soy sauce 2 tbsp. honey

× 2 tsp. rice-wine vinegar 1/2 tsp.g rated ginger

× 1/2 tsp. oriental sesame oil Pinch of cayenne

× 1 tsp. sesame seeds

× 1 tbsp. chopped fresh coriander or parsley

directions

1. Remove the wing tips and cut them in half at the joint. Chop the garlic and chives.

2. Combine soy sauce, honey, vinegar, garlic, ginger, oil, and cayenne pepper in a microwave-safe dish.

3. Add wings and flip to coat.

4. Marinate for at least 30 minutes, turning twice.

5. Put larger wings on the edge of the plate.

6. Cover with plastic and ventilate. Cook in the microwave on high for 5 minutes.

7. Turn the plate over and cook 5 more minutes. Transfer the wings to a serving plate. Return the marinade to the oven and cook, partially covered, over high heat for 2 minutes.

8. Pour the marinade over the wings and flip to coat.

9. Sprinkle with sesame seeds, chives, and coriander. 12 pieces.

CHICKEN CASSEROLE

ingredients

- × 1 (2-2 1/2 lbs.) chicken, boiled and off bone
- × 1 can cream of mushroom soup
- × 1 can cream of chicken soup
- × 1 (8 oz.) sour cream
- × 1 (8 oz.) Cheez Whiz
- × 1 stick butter or margarine
- × 1 1/2 sleeves of Ritz crackers or saltines Poppy seeds

directions

1. Place bite-sized pieces of chicken in bottom of 9 x 13-inch pan.

2. Combine soups (undiluted), sour cream, and Cheez Whiz in a medium bowl.

3. Put this mixture on top of the chicken.

4. Sprinkle poppy seeds over the soup mix.

5. Melt stick of butter. Crush the cookies.

6. Toss, then sprinkle evenly over the chicken casserole.

7. Bake in 350 degree oven for 20-30 minutes, until bubbly and golden brown. Serves 6. This is a family favorite!

FRIED CHICKEN BREAST

ingredients

- × 2 Boneless chicken breasts (can also use 1 turkey breast)
- × 1 c. all-purpose flour
- × 1 tbsp. paprika
- × 4 tsp. salt
- × 1/2 tsp. pepper
- × 2 c. bread crumbs
- × 2 eggs
- × 1/2 c. milk

directions

1. Heat 1 inch of salad oil to 370 degrees.

2. Cut the chicken into strips.

3. Combine the flour, paprika, salt, and pepper in one bowl and the breadcrumbs in another.

4. Mix the eggs and milk.

5. Dip the chicken in the flour mixture, then the egg mixture, and then the breadcrumbs.

6. Fry a few pieces at a time for 3 to 5 minutes, until tender.

7. Drain on paper towels.

CHICKEN IN THE GARDEN

ingredients

× Aluminum foil

× Ready to cook chicken pieces Sm. potatoes

× Cherry tomatoes Med. onions Fresh mushrooms Green peppers

× Worcestershire sauce Salt, pepper, paprika Butter or margarine

directions

1. Cut 40-inch pieces of aluminum foil for each dinner guest. Fold the aluminum foil in half.

2. Place the chicken, potato, tomato, onion, mushrooms, and green pepper on foil.

3. Sprinkle with Worcestershire, salt, pepper, and paprika. Sprinkle with butter. Fold the aluminum foil. Bake in 450 degree oven (in a shallow skillet) about an hour or cook over fired charcoal. Turn the package over every 20 to 30 minutes.

CHICKEN PARISIENNE

ingredients

- × 4-6 lg. chicken breasts
- × 1 can condensed cream of mushroom soup
- × 3 oz. (2/3 c.) mushrooms, with liquid
- × 1 c. dairy sour cream
- × 1/2 c.
- × Cooking sherry or white wine Paprika

directions

1. Place chicken breast in 11 x 7 x 1 1/2 inch baking dish.

2. Combine sour cream, cream of mushroom soup, mushrooms, and sherry and pour over chicken.

3. Sprinkle generously with paprika.

4. Bake at 350 degrees for about 1 to 1 1/4 hours or until tender. Serve with warm fluffy rice.

LEMON CHICKEN SAUCE

ingredients

- × 4 1/2 tbsp. sugar
- × 4 1/2 tbsp. lemon juice
- × 4 1/2 tbsp. chicken stock
- × 3/4 tsp. salt
- × 2 tsp. cornstarch
- × 1 1/2 tsp. sesame oil
- × 1 1/2 tsp. yellow food coloring (optional) Rind from lemon
- × Several drops lemon extract

directions

1. Cook sauce until thick over high heat, stirring constantly.

2. Pour sauce over cooked chicken pieces. Serve hot.

ORIENTAL CHICKEN TENDERS CURRIED PEANUT CHICKEN (variation)

ingredients

- × 4 halves, skinned & boned chicken breasts 2 c. half & half
- × 1 1/2 c. mayonnaise
- × 3 tbsp. mango chutney 2 tbsp. dry sherry
- × 1 tbsp. sherry vinegar
- × 2 tbsp. plus 1 tsp. curry powder 1 tsp. turmeric
- × 2 c. finely chopped salted roasted peanuts

directions

1. Preheat the oven to 350 degrees.

2. Place the chicken breasts in a shallow baking dish large enough to contain them.

3. Pour half and half over them and bake for 30 minutes.

4. Let cool and cut into 1-inch cubes.

5. Process mayonnaise, hot sauce, sherry, vinegar, curry powder, and turmeric in a blender or food processor.

6. Dip the chicken pieces in the curry mayonnaise and roll in the chopped walnuts. Refrigerate 30 minutes.

7. Arrange on a serving plate with fancy toothpicks.

CHICKEN WINGS

ingredients

- × 36 chicken wings
- × 1 (5 oz.) bottle soy sauce
- × 1 tsp. Dijon mustard
- × 4 tbsp.
- × Brown sugar
- × 1/2 tsp. garlic powder

directions

1. Rinse chicken wings and pat dry.

2. Mix soy sauce, mustard, brown sugar and garlic powder together.

3. Marinate wings in mixture overnight (or about 6 hours).

4. Bake wings on cookie sheet for about 1 hour at 375 degrees. Baste wings occasionally with sauce. Serves 9-12.

HOT-N-SPICY CHICKEN WINGS

ingredients

- × 5 lbs. bag chicken wings (drumettes)
- × 12 fl. oz. Louisiana Pre Crystal Hot Sauce
- × 1-2 sticks butter

directions

1. Fry chicken wings until golden brown and drain on paper towel.

2. Mix hot sauce and melted butter and pour into deep pan or crock pot.

3. Add chicken wings to sauce and heat thoroughly.

SPICY CHICKEN WINGS

ingredients

- × 1 lg. can Parmesan cheese
- × 2 tbsp. oregano
- × 4 tbsp. parsley
- × 1 tsp. salt
- × 1 tsp. pepper
- × 1 stick margarine
- × 4-5 lbs. chicken wings

directions

1. Line a cookie sheet with aluminum foil.

2. Melt the margarine in a small saucepan.

3. Cut the chicken wings. Discard the tips.

4. Mix all the dry ingredients in a bowl. Dip the chicken wings in margarine and roll in the cheese mixture.

5. Place on a cookie sheet.

6. Bake in preheated 350 degree oven for 1 hour. Serve hot.

CRISPY ORIENTAL CHICKEN WINGS (MICROWAVE)

ingredients

- × 1 1/2 lbs. chicken wings,
- × disjointed 1 med. egg
- × 1/2 c. soy sauce
- × 2 tbsp. garlic powder
- × 1/4 tsp. ginger powder
- × 1 med. onion, finely diced
- × 2 c. finely crushed corn flakes

directions

1. Mix in the egg, soy sauce, garlic powder, and ginger powder.

2. Set aside. On wax paper, mix together the crushed cornflakes and the diced onion.

3. Dip each wing in the soy sauce mixture, then roll in corn flakes and onion. In a glass baking dish, cover and cook the wings on high (9) for 20 minutes or until done.

4. Remove the lid halfway through cooking.

5. Use a 13x9 "baking dish.

TERIYAKI CHICKEN WINGS

ingredients

- × 1/3 c. lemon juice
- × 1/4 c. soy sauce
- × 1/4 c. vegetable oil
- × 3 tbsp. chili sauce
- × 1 clove garlic, finely chopped
- × 1/4 tsp. pepper
- × 1/4 tsp. celery seed Dash of dry mustard
- × 3 lb. chicken wings

directions

1. MARINADE: Combine lemon juice, soy sauce, oil, hot sauce, garlic, pepper, celery seed, and mustard.

2. Stir well, set aside.

3. Cut the chicken wings at the joint and remove the wing tips.

4. Place the chicken in a baking dish.

5. Pour the marinade over the chicken.

6. Cover, refrigerate at least 4 hours or overnight.

7. Drain and place on a roasting pan. Grill about 10 minutes on each side with the pan about 7 inches from the heating element. Brush occasionally with the marinade.

Anatomy of the Chicken

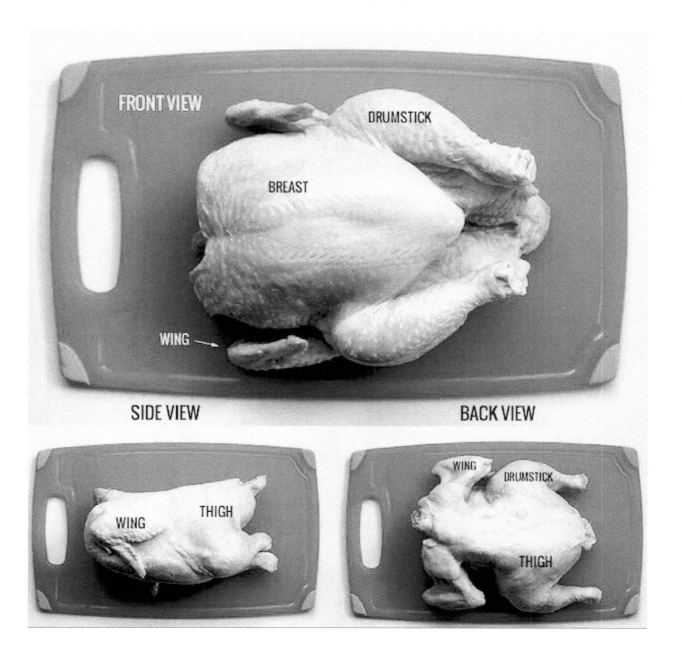

ANATOMY OF THE CHICKEN

Head

The head is the talkie part of South Africa's famous walkie-talkies and stewing and braising are the best ways to cook it.

Breast

This very lean cut is best cooked quickly to keep them moist, for instance grilling, frying and braaiing. When stewing for braising breasts, don't overcook them as they will become dry and stringy.

Wing

Wings are high in fat and can withstand heat without becoming dry. They therefore are suited to deep- frying, braaiing and roasting. But however you cook them,

Tail

TAILS The tail is often attached to the thigh. It is packed with flavour because it contains a lot of fat and, thanks to the large skin area, becomes very crispy.

ANATOMY OF THE CHICKEN

Neck

This bony cut has very little meat but is an inexpensive way to flavour sauces and stock.

Thighs

Like drumsticks, thighs will be rather tough if not cooked properly. They have loads of fantastic flavour and are best when roasted or braised slowly or added to stews.

Drumstic

This popular cut could also be tough if it hasn't been cooked for long enough. The delicious dark brown meat particularly takes time and drumsticks taste best when they've been roasted, stewed, braised or braaied.

Feet

The other half of walkie-talkies, chicken feet are bony and low on meat. Once cooked, though, they are tender and can be eaten whole. Braai or grill them if you like crisp, crunchy skin.

HOW MANY CALORIES IN CHICKEN?

Chicken tenders

263 calories per 3.5 ounces (100 grams)

Back

137 calories per 3.5 ounces (100 grams)

Dark meat

125 calories per 3.5 ounces (100 grams)

Light meat

114 calories per 3.5 ounces (100 grams)

HOW MANY CALORIES IN CHICKEN?

Breast

A 3.5-ounce (100-gram) serving of chicken breast provides 165 calories, 31 grams of protein and 3.6 grams of fat.

Thigh

A 3.5-ounce (100-gram) serving of chicken thigh provides 209 calories, 26 grams of protein and 10.9 grams of fat.

Wing

Per 3.5 ounces (100 grams), chicken wings provide 203 calories, 30.5 grams of protein and 8.1 grams of fat.

Drumstick

Per 3.5 ounces (100 grams), chicken drumsticks have 172 calories, 28.3 grams of protein and 5.7 grams of fat.

Skin

While a skinless chicken breast is 284 calories with 80% protein and 20% fat, those numbers **dramatically** shift when you include the skin. One boneless, cooked chicken breast with skin (196 grams) contains: Calories: 386, Protein: 58.4 grams, Fat: 15.2 grams

COOKING METHODS

Grilling

This is one of the more common cooking methods, as it tends to require less added fat.

Baking or roasting

These other common methods are sufficient when you don't have access to a grill.

Broiling

This is similar to grilling, but you usually do it in a standard oven or toaster oven.

Braising

Lightly panfry the chicken and then cook it covered, submerged in liquid, for an extended time at a lower temperature.

COOKING METHODS

Fried

The chicken is submerged in hot cooking oil in either a pan or deep fryer. This creates a crisp outer coating but adds quite a bit of fat.

Baking or roasting

These other common methods are sufficient when you don't have access to a grill.

Boiling

You submerge the meat in boiling water and cook it until the internal temperature reaches 165°F (74°C). This is the leanest method, as it doesn't require added fats. Still, some may find the texture lacking.

Quick Recipes

Lemon Garlic Chicken

Place whole roasting chicken in baker with one whole lemon and one head of garlic (unpeeled) in cavity of chicken. Season with salt and pepper. Cover with lid and cook for 1-1/2 hours at 425°. (Try with an orange too.)

Roasted Turkey Breast

Place turkey breast in baker; place 6-8 small red skinned potatoes, halved, around turkey. Add 1/2 cup white wine and 2 cloves pressed garlic. Season with salt and pepper. Cover with lid. Bake at 350°F for 1-1/2 hours. Uncover for last 15-20 minutes. Let stand 5 minutes before slicing.

Honey Mustard Chicken

Place roasting chicken in the baker and pour fat free honey mustard dressing over the top. Cover with lid. Roast for 1-1/2 hours at 425°F.

3 CHEFS' TIPS
A little know-how can make life in the kitchen a lot easier

Done Yet

There are two ways to check if a chicken breast is done.
The first is to insert the tip of a small knife into the thickest part of the meat. If the juices run clear, it is cooked; if it's still pink,
you need to cook longer. Alternatively, make a small incision in the thickest part of the breast. If the meat is completely white and you don't see any pink meat, the brisket is done. The juices will also be clear. This method also works for testing whole chickens and other chicken pieces.

Slicing chicken breast for stir fry

Place the chicken breast, smooth-side down on a cutting board.
Cut it diagonally into 1 cm strips and halve each strip lengthwise into longer, thinner strips before cutting them diagonally across the fibres to keep it tender.

Butterflying chicken breasts for schnitzels

Place the chicken breast smooth side down on a cutting board. Make a shallow incision along one side and continue as if you were trying to cut the breast into two identical halves. Stop just before cutting it all the way through, so the top and bottom half open like a book. With a meat mallet, tap the thickest part gently until it is finer and more uniform. Butterfly breasts can also be stuffed with any filling you like.

TIPS AND TRICKS

Keeping it Clean

- × Once chicken has been defrosted, do not refreeze it.
- × Don't let raw chicken come into contact with other food, cooked or un-cooked.
- × Always wash your hands, utensils and surfaces that have been in contact with raw chicken with hot, soapy water.
- × Keep a separate chopping board for raw meat to prevent cross-contamination.
- × Always make sure that meat is cooked through to kill all harmful bacteria that may have been lurking in it.

When buying chicken

Always look for chicken that has an even colour with no blemishes or bruises. The meat should look moist and plump and have a neutral smell. Check that the packaging hasn't been damaged in any way. When buying frozen chicken, make sure that the meat is frozen solid and does not have any soft areas where it has begun to defrost – and do remember to check the sell-by-date too.

Storing Chicken

Always refrigerate or freeze chicken as soon as possible after purchasing it. If the package is damaged or soggy and you are going to cook it within two days, remove the chicken, pat dry with kitchen paper, and place on a plate. Cover with cling film or aluminum foil and place plate on bottom rack of refrigerator. That way you won't contaminate other food if it leaks. If you want to freeze the chicken at home, remove it from the package, pat dry, and seal it in an airtight bag.

TIPS AND TRICKS

Stop Breast Drying

How to stop the breast from drying out when MAKING roast chicken.
Roast the chicken breast-side down for two thirds of the cooking time. This way, all the juices will run down into the breast meat and keep it moist. Once you are ready to crisp the skin, carefully turn the chicken breast-side up and roast until golden.

How Tos and Hacks

Chicken salad. Place chicken breast side up on cutting board. Pull the
the leg and thigh away from the body and use your fingers to find the hip joint in the crease. Insert the tip of a large knife into the joint and cut through the skin, meat, and joint to separate the thigh and leg from the body. Repeat on the other side. Use the same method to separate the leg from the thigh and cut the wings from the body. To remove the chicken breast, cut the breast to divide the carcass in two. Cut all the bone and cartilage from the breasts.
You will now have two of each: thighs, drumsticks, wings, and breasts. Add the carcass to soups, stews or casseroles for flavor and remove the bones just before serving.

How to defrost a whole chicken

Thawing a frozen chicken is best done overnight in the fridge. Place it in a large bowl or on a plate to prevent the juices from dripping in the fridge. Before cooking it, check inside the cavity to see that there is no more ice. If pressed for time, put the bird in a bucket of cold water in the sink, but be sure to keep the water cold to prevent bacteria from growing.

TIPS AND TRICKS

Getting a golden skin

Check that the skin is completely dry, rub the whole bird generously with oil and season well.
Uncover the chicken 20-30 minutes before the end of the cooking time and place it on a shallow baking tray or on an oven rack on a tray to allow the dry heat to come into contact with as much skin as possible. Roast until the skin is crisp and glassy

Chicken and food poisoning

Raw chicken may contain natural bacteria, which could be dangerous if it hasn't been stored properly. Salmonella and campylobacter, which are linked to food poisoning and gastro, are among the most common.

3 DIPS FOR CHICKEN NUGGETS

Garlic and lemon mayo

Stir 2 finely chopped garlic cloves and zest and juice of 1/2 lemon into 1 cup (250 ml) Mayonnaise.

Tomato relish

Finely chop 3 small sherkins and 3 pickeled onions and stir into 3/4 cup (180ml) tomato sauce.

Sweet and sour

Stir together 3/4 cup (180 ml) pineapple juice, 1/4 cup (60 ml) apple cider vinegar, 1/4 cup (60 ml) brown sugar, 2 tbsp (30 ml) tomato cauce and 1 tbps (15 ml) cornflour. Thicker over a low heat.

Quick Recipes

Chicken Pot Pie

Simmer a couple of boneless, skinless chicken breasts, let cool and cube. Microwave cubed potatoes, carrots, celery, onion, green beans or peas. Combine with cornstarch-thickened chicken broth (from the simmered chicken), and pour into pie crust lined baker (you can use Pillsbury ready made) then top with the other crust, crimp, brush with milk, sprinkle with herbs, sesame seeds, or a little Parmesan, and bake at 350° about 40 min.

Cranberry Chicken

Mix one can of whole berry cranberries w/ can of cream of mushroom soup and one packet of onion soup mix. Pour over top of chicken in baker. Cover with lid, place in oven; bake for 1-1/2 hours at 425.

Chicken and Vegetables

Place chicken (skin on or off) in baker. Place chopped onion, celery and carrots around chicken. Sprinkle with 1/2 package of Good Seasons Italian Dressing mix. Place lid on top. Bake at 350° for 1 hour.